"During the last seven years, I have the privilege of witnessing John Kuek's commitment to serve political refugees and immigrants from Africa. His book is a testimony of his awareness, knowledge and skills addressing the needs of his community and a guide for the implementation of culturally competent mental health and social services."

Sonia Carbonell. PsyD # 1972
Clinical and Cultural Psychologist
Centro de Psychologies Cultural

I0441937

"John Kuek is a brilliant, stalwart scholar whose ideas have revolutionized the future of the Sudanese Community. His great knowledge in Psychology and years of experience in counseling will ad-infinitum and influence the positive social changes in Sudanese Community as well as in the larger scope of the entire world community. His book will, of course, assist immigrants to implicit their cosmopolitan amalgamations in North America."

Koang G. Bidit
Doctor of Philosophy (Ph.D.)
Student: PPA - Law and Public Policy, Walden University
Master of Public Administration (M.P.A.), National University
B.S. in Computer Information Systems, National University.

"I have had the pleasure of knowing John Kuek for a long time, having worked with him as his employer, trainer, and manager. He was enrolled in college at my recommendation and has exceled in all areas. John is a very hard working fellow who also aims at achieving the maximum efficiency in all of the possible areas of work that he handles. He puts his whole self into the task that has been assigned. A knowledge thirsty person, he is always ready to learn and know more about things and is always up to achieving complete mastery over his work. John is an intelligent, capable, dedicated, and personable man. He is always quick on his feet, with sensible reactions in all the circumstances I have witnessed. I feel confident in saying that he is capable person."

Gabaynesh Galila Gashaw-Gant, Psy.D.
Director of Ethiopia, Eritrean, Somalia, and Sudan in Africa (ESSEA) Incorporated.

"...Great insight into South Sudanese culture, trauma, and healing."

Zara Marselian, President/CEO
La Maestra Community Health Centers

"I was very impressed with the 'emotional power' and relevance of this book to the struggles of peoples from all over the world who are trying to find a niche in life and reaching a sense of belonging. I endorse this book with no reservations!"

Roberto J. Velasquez, Ph.D.
Retired Professor of Psychology
San Diego State University and Director
Family Wellness Program
La Maestra Community Health Centers
San Diego, California

South Sudanese Community Insights

A Cross-Generational Cross-Cultural Rescue Model for Families and Family Counselors

by John Chuol Kuek

Copyright © 2012
by John Chuol Kuek

All rights reserved. No part of this book may be reproduced or transmitted in any form or by any means, electronic or mechanical, including photocopying, recording, or by any information storage and retrieval system, without written permission from the author, except for the inclusion of brief quotations in a review that includes proper accreditation.

DISCLAIMER:
This book contains the opinions and ideas of the author and is intended for informational purposes only. It is not intended to serve as a substitute for professional medical advice. Any product mentioned in this book does not imply endorsement of that product by the author or publisher. It is sold with the understanding that the author and publisher are not engaged in rendering medical, health, psychological or any other kind of personal professional services in the book.

The author and publisher specifically disclaim all responsibility for any liability, loss or risk, personal or otherwise, that is incurred as a consequence, directly or indirectly, of the use and application of the contents of this book. While the author and publisher have used their best efforts in preparing this book, they make no representations or warranties with respect to the accuracy or completeness of the contents of this book and specifically disclaim any implied warranties or merchantability or fitness for a particular purpose. No warranty may be created or extended by sales representatives or written sales materials. The advice and strategies contained herein may not be suitable for your situation. You should consult with a professional where appropriate. Neither the publisher nor author shall be liable for any loss or profit or any other commercial damages, including but not limited to special, incidental, consequential or other damages.

South Sudanese Community Insights: A Cross-Generational Cross-Cultural Rescue Model for Families and Family Counselors
by John Chuol Kuek with Walter Davis, Jr.

Library of Congress Catalog Card Number

International Standard Book Number
978-1530171897

Printed in the United States of America

Table of Contents

Dedication

I dedicate this book to my late uncle, a person I refer to as a best friend, my mentor, and a community leader, John Jock Kang. He supported and encouraged me to excel to this level. John Kang was one of the few founders of the Sudanese Community Association, the local non-profit organization established to serve the needs of the newly arrived Sudanese refugees and immigrants in San Diego.

The Sudanese Community Association helps new arrivals connect with employment agencies and adjust to the challenges of life in their new homeland. John Kang worked for La Maestra Community Health Centers as an employment counselor. He had served as an educational counselor as well to the young refugees and immigrants who wished to continue their education in the United States' educational system. He helped guide them with career choices and employment.

John Kang was a pastor of the Sudanese Fellowship at the College Center Covenant Church until he passed away. John Kang had also served as a cultural and political historian to the Sudanese community, and he had been a tremendous help to me in serving the community as well. Included in this acknowledgement is his quote while he was at the Mercy Hospital, seven days before he passed away on September 15, 2005. He was speaking with Sylva Jurish about the possibility of me joining him to work at the La Maestra Community Health Centers. "John Kuek already works fulltime and goes to school twice a week at 5:00 PM after work. La Maestra schedule is 9:00 AM to 6:00PM, so I do not want to interrupt his school because he is the future of our community. Even if I do not continue to live, John Kuek will service our community just like I have done. My only worry is that he will be overwhelmed by many issues that he and I have been handling together, side by side, but he will be fine." I have achieved this now with his support.

Acknowledgements

I would like to thank a few individuals who have had significant impact on my personal and professional life. In many respects, these are the people who have not only influenced my thoughts, but have also given me much personal support. First and foremost is my family: My lovely wife Rebecca Nyaret Koda and my beautiful children who have been my inspiration to accomplish this goal. My mother Nyayul Kun Gai Kuoth, my sister Sarah Nyayien Kuek and her husband James Lam Gatluak, my lovely younger sister Roda Nyapuot Kuek and her husband David Kueth Yul plus their children have given me support I needed and have been the backbone of this accomplishment. My late mother in-law Nyantut Toang Duach had played a crucial role in my education by providing childcare while both my wife and I were busy with school and work. My brother in-law Jacob Koang Koda and his family have given my family major support to make sure we stay bounded in this Cultural Revolution.

I wish to thank my friend Walter Davis for his many hours editing this book, and for connecting me to Marilyn McLeod who has helped to make my dream come true in publishing this, my very first book, "South Sudanese Community Insights: A Cross-Generational Cross-Cultural Rescue Model for Families and Family Counselors." I also appreciate Walter's tireless work for the South Sudanese Community Center. In addition I am indebted to my South Sudanese Community and the Nuer Community of San Diego in particular for standing behind me to make our community a loving model for change to the Nuer Community worldwide.

Thanks to Dr. Gebaynesh Galilia Gashaw-Gant for her outstanding leadership in the community and being my role model in the mental health profession. Without her support and example, I wouldn't be in this field of behavioral health profession, so I count on her for much educational advice.

My biggest and best thanks goes to my clinical supervisor, Linda Gallegos, for making sure that I gain the knowledge needed to provide quality service to the community. Appreciation goes as well to my best friends, Elena Cruz and Dr. Sonia Carbonell for being there rallying behind me to boost my self-confident in the mental health profession, and to Diana Alvarez for professional assistance in my MFT accreditation process.

My deepest gratitude goes to my employer, La Maestra Community Health Centers in general, and to my dear friends on the administration department, Zara Marselian, Elizabeth David, Alejandrina Areizaga, and Alexei Ochola for providing me a safe atmosphere suitable for growth in this profession. It wouldn't have been possible for me to excel to this level without their support. Last, but not least, is my dear friend, Sylva Jurich for her dedicated service to the Sudanese community. With her support, I became part of the La Maestra Community Health Centers.

Foreword

While I was filming and streaming a webcast of a graduation ceremony to Africa, a young man appeared with a cap and gown. I was drawn to his brilliant smile, pleasant personality and intelligent conversation. I learned that this dynamic man was John Kuek. He had just earned his master's degree. As we interacted more, I learned that we had much in common. I grew to love and respect him as a brother. This book is a product of our collaboration on many projects.

This book may appear to present strange concepts at first glance, if read from a western-centric view point. When I first heard some of them, I experienced humor, confusion and epiphany. Close inspection reveals an opportunity for the enlightened to be further enlightened. Is it better to pay thousands of dollars to have strangers resolve family disputes as it is done in the west or better to have elders in the family resolve marital discord as is common in the South Sudanese culture? Is the reality of a "Secret Boyfriend" unique to only the South Sudanese culture or, is it simply acknowledged differently? These and other cultural aspects warrant deep introspect.

The clash between traditional South Sudanese values and western values threatens the survival of families already rocked by decades of war, poverty and injustice. Outsiders will get a glimpse into the South Sudanese family. One can see how western values affect the relationships between youth and their parents. The unique value of uncles and elders in the South Sudanese culture is beautifully described by John.

Social workers, therapists and other public officials can get a better understanding of the inner dynamics involved in the South Sudanese mindset. This understanding is integral to the administration of effective therapy and dispensing of justice to South Sudanese families that have experienced far too little of both.

This book provides powerful tools with which the South Sudanese people can experience an epiphany. With this, they can begin to gain insight into how their traditional values are being affected by diasporas. This book provides a path to family healing. It provides an opportunity for a more effective metamorphosis with regard to the inevitable blending of cultures and tribal outlooks. South Sudanese people can become acquainted with the value of treatment to help assuage the effects of decades of war, loss and tribal resentments. The energy expended within internal quarrels can be refocused by South Sudanese community leaders to manage the monumental challenges facing their communities.

This book provides us all with an insight of how to be more self-reflective, compassionate and open-minded. John Kuek's masterful and almost musical use of language provides an easy to read roadmap to a more loving future.

John Kuek's unique insight into South Sudan culture and the west reveals an intelligent work. This book is a must read for anyone interacting with the South Sudan population in either a public or private capacity.

Walter Davis
Writer, Producer, Director

Introduction

Purpose

This book has been written for three groups of people and issues: (1) South Sudanese couples who were born, grew up and married in South Sudan, (2) young Sudanese couples and adolescents whom were born and grew up in refugee camps and the western world, who have not had a chance to experience a typical South Sudanese cultural way of life and therefore have hard times juggling between the three cultures (refugee camp, the South Sudanese and the Western World) in terms of raising their families, and (3) the behavioral health or mental health professionals serving the Sudanese and other groups whose cultures are similar to the South Sudanese worldwide.

This book has seven purposes: (1) to explore the impact of cultural change on the South Sudanese marriage couples, not only in the Western world, but also in Africa, (2) explore the impact of separation and divorce on the South Sudanese's single parents and their children and the role of child support on the absent parent, (3) the change of the South Sudanese's marriage system as a result of an impact of the cultural revolution in the West, (4) the role of American's domestic violence laws on the Sudanese families, (5) the bigger picture of the South Sudanese's problem worldwide, (6) offer step-by-step education to help reduce the high risk of losing their cultural values, preventing mental health risk as a result of being overwhelmed with staggering issues, and help get the best out of the US educational system, not only for their benefits, but also for the benefits of those in the new born country, the Republic of South Sudan, (7) assist the behavioral or mental health professionals involved in counseling the South Sudanese and other groups with similar culture and behavior, with appropriate education to provide competent services.

Background

The typical South Sudanese values and the way of life have changed tremendously from the refugee camps. Life in the refugee camps have traumatized this generation and completely changed their behaviors. I was born and raised in South Sudan. I joined the displaced South Sudanese refugee camp at Itang refugee camp in Ethiopia, in 1987 at age 15. I had an opportunity to start my education there. The refugee camp was very crowded with a variety of South Sudanese tribes. There were up to eight hundred thousand people with no clean water, one medical clinic, one primary school, and a military training camp for white army recruits. In addition many people were able to join the church with an intention to transform their lives through Christianity and education. Many prayers were offered for peace in the hope they could return to South Sudan. Many children and adults perished in the camps in large numbers due to the many communicable diseases such as typhoid, cholera, yellow fever, measles, hepatitis, tuberculosis and meningitis, just to name a few.

Medical help was lacking, with only one or two doctors serving eight hundred thousand people plus. Eight hundred thousand people were sustained by the United Nations' world food program. South Sudanese community members saw their traditional values and dignity began to erode in the camps. Many who had the chance to step into leadership roles of food distribution demonstrated a bad example as they took advantage of the larger population by distributing only part of the food and selling the rest to Ethiopian merchants for their individual benefit.

The majority of those living in the camp had never experienced city life before arriving in camp. Some of the villagers learned to read and write in the camp, and they gained leadership roles. New arrivals to the camp became inspired to become leaders as they observed the value of education. Camp residents competed to attend school in order to lead just like those individuals who became wealthy in the camp because of their educational and leadership advantage.

In addition to the bad example shown by the refugee leaders, military officers from the movement also demonstrated non-transparent leadership and traumatized the ordinary Sudanese. For instance, the South Sudanese's marriage had never been as easy as the military officers used it. They would take a cow by force from civilians and use them as a dowry to marry their daughters. This is a clear violation of the norms of this culture and a traumatizing situation at the same time. They often selectively married the most beautiful girls using valuable cows and money collected from the ordinary South Sudanese. The Nuer were especially vulnerable because they bordered Ethiopia refugee and military training camps. Many married up to 15 wives or more. The innocent and uneducated South Sudanese viewed this leadership style as oppressive and felt imposed upon.

The great struggle on so many fronts traumatized many. The way South Sudanese were accustomed to living their lives was changed. After witnessing this behavior in multiple refugee camps and seeing the manifestation of that behavior in the Sudanese community of the United States, I realized that the community needed to change course toward a healthy direction. Further, South Sudanese people living in South Sudan and government officials noticed this problem as well; they were unsure of what to do about it.

In search of the answer, some Sudanese and Nuer figures have stepped forward and spoken openly about these problems. Among the pioneers in this struggle is uncle Thowath Pal Chay, a Nuer Ethiopian political dissident and Dr. Riek Machar Teny, the Vice President of the Republic of South Sudan. Their opinions and others are well documented in Chapter 3 of this book. Like these pioneers, I have been thinking of a way to address these challenges with a hope to turn this community around. Since I came to this country and observed the behavior of South Sudanese people in social interactions, I have seen the need for healing. My long standing dream resulted in this book addressing the enormous issues in diasporas as well as in the newly formed country, the Republic of South Sudan.

Overview

The chapters that follow reflect the insight I have gathered on the South Sudanese community at home and abroad. There is a challenge to the leadership in our government, community, churches, and families which requires attention. The format of the book therefore is straight forward. Each chapter identifies an issue integral to the task of community creation and nurturing of prospective leaders. In the first chapter, I explore practices of marriage in context of culture, Nuer historical facts and the Nuer culture in particular. The second chapter examines the practices of marriage partner selection; the entire chapter is devoted to pre-marital education for teenagers or youth. The chapter reflects the Secret of Family Happiness (1996) as it relates to the culture and system of the South Sudanese marriages.

In the third chapter, I explore South Sudanese over-arching issues including family crisis description, domestic violence and US laws. Suggestions for resolving these issues are included. They focus on the development of new ideas in the community conversation as they relate to the principles of good governance, education, and administrative realities of Sudanese people worldwide.

The fourth chapter offers an alternative way of critical thinking. Included are practical steps toward resolving the crisis. This chapter supports concepts explored in chapters one and two. There is a focus on education in reference to modern realities. Expert advisors reflect on systematic and well established models. The intention is to help the nation to "reconcile" with one another as the Vice President of the Republic of South Sudan, Dr. Riek Machar voiced in a phone conversation.

The fifth chapter contains references. Tribal differences, political differences, and clannish behaviors are all products of the Sudanese culture. Political leaders, church leaders, and head of the families are hampered by these components in a challenge of creating a loveable community of faith. Nearly all community and political leaders with whom I talked emphasized frustration from their efforts to effect change. The leadership in the South Sudanese community has failed to develop visions, resources, or leadership training programs that promote practices integral to healthy families, worship, education, mission focus, and effective administration. They have failed to develop effective responses to the multi-tribal and diverse ethnicities they seek to embrace. This book seeks to bridge the divisions in the current South Sudanese community.

Wendy James, a former student of Sir Edward Evans-Pritchard, recommends several texts to help one grasp the situation. The book (Kinship and Marriage Among the Nuer, first printed in 1951 and second printed in the 1990s), Douglas H. Johnson, History and Prophecy among the Nuer of the South Sudan (UCLA Ph.D. thesis, 1980); Gabriel Giet Jal, The History of the Jikany Nuer before 1920 (University of London Ph.D. thesis, 1987); Sharon E. Hutchinson, The Nuer in Crisis: Coping with Money, War and the State (University of Chicago Ph.D. thesis, 1988). It is my pleasure to incorporate these great authors in my book as an honor to their great work that reflects the Nuer history and life.

About the Author

John Chuol Kuek earned a BA in Psychology, M.S in Counseling, and a Ph.D. Advanced Candidate in Psychology. John has become the first East African culturally appropriate therapist in San Diego County. He is currently working as a Marriage and Family Therapist Intern, pursuing his licensing process to become a licensed Marriage and Family Therapist. As the first East African Therapist, John has been providing therapy to families, individuals, children, couples ... and more ... with psychological issues from all walks of life.

John served on the Board of Directors of the Sudanese Community Association of San Diego as a General Secretary from 1999-2003. John also served on the board of the Southern Sudanese Community Center of San Diego from 2009-present. He was elected Chairman of the Board of Directors and is currently serving his term. In addition to serving at the leadership level of this community based organization, he is also serving as a church minister for the Sudanese Fellowship of the College Center Evangelical Covenant Church.

From 2000-2001 John started working as a Community Health Advocate with the New Americans Health Advocacy Program of Project Concern International's California Initiative, which aims to bridge the cultural and linguistic gaps of accessing health care and education for East African immigrants and refugees in San Diego. John worked to bridge the cultural differences and language barriers, helping his community find and utilize health services, and provide basic health education and referrals. John's interest in health, his outgoing personality and his enthusiasm were a tremendous asset to this program.

From 2001-2006 John worked as a project coordinator for Project ESSEA, the Ethiopian, Sudanese, Somalian, and Eritrean in Africa, a behavioral health project founded by Dr. Gebaynesh Galila Gashaw-Gant. The program aims to serve the needs of the East African population by providing a therapeutic approach which is flexible and culturally appropriate. In addition, there is a goal of providing educational materials and outreach efforts that de-emphasize the stigma associated with behavioral health problems and treatment. Through his work with this project, he became interested in changing his career from nursing to psychology. John's passion has always been to service the needs of people in one way or another.

From 1998-2001 John worked as a certified nursing assistant (CNA) for Internext Home Care, which became Front Porch Home Care, a Retirement Communities facility in San Diego, California. John gained an interest in the health field as a result of his work with an International Non-Governmental Organization in Ethiopia's Itang refugee camp, providing interpretation between Ethiopian doctors and the Sudanese patients.

Overall, his love for helping others in any capacity is a characteristic that differentiates him from others. His hard work and ability to cross boundaries to build capacity with others in the community is unsurpassed. His devoted service has gained him the respect and appreciation of his fellow workers and other professionals who have worked with him. John is committed to each individual within the larger community. His capacity to provide information and advice in the specialized field of human service lets him conduct business in a highly effective manner.

Walter Davis, Jr. and John Kuek served on the Board of Directors of the South Sudanese Community Center of San Diego.

Walter was shaped by the civil rights era in which he grew up and has suffered much personal grief but always managed to find a positive path to follow. A Navy veteran with 25 years service, Walter is also a lifelong student, constantly learning and reinventing himself.

Walter is a Web Videographer/Media Consultant/Executive Producer Public Access TV/ Columnist with more than 30 years experience with Internet media. Mr. Davis is capable of interviewing people from anywhere in the world via Internet TV and Radio. He has trained more than 300 people to produce their own shows. He currently produces six television shows on COX communications reaching San Diego, Imperial and Riverside Counties, California. He owns and operates ten Internet TV channels and one Internet radio channel. He was the first to webcast Public Access TV shows live on three Internet TV channels and Internet Radio simultaneously. His column Left Hook displays progressive values in conservative papers and can be found in The Rancho Bernardo Sun and East County Magazine.

A retired Navy navigator and Harpoon Cruise Missile Engagement Officer, Mr. Davis served in Surface Action Groups in all five of the United States Navy's active fleets. A combat veteran with tours including Drug and Slave interdiction in South and Central America and The Strait of Malacca; combat action in Bosnia, Libya, Israel, Lebanon, and the North Arabian Sea; eleven deployments in six warships. As a Naval Warfare Operations Specialist, he began working with the World Wide Military Command and Control System in 1976 the predecessor of The Internet.

Ashore, Senior Chief Davis served as a Chemical Dependency specialist, specializing in the treatment of alcohol, cocaine and steroid addiction. He has traveled the world delivering lectures on chemical addiction for the Navy Department as well as civilian agencies including the Drug Policy Alliance and HealthNet. After 25 years of service, he retired in 2001 as a Southern California Anti-Terrorism Coordinator at San Diego's Space and Naval Warfare Systems Command.

After his pregnant wife and little girl were gunned down in Los Angeles in 1989 and the insurance company did not pay health and death benefits to his family, he started his own insurance brokerage AgentOnWheels.com. He specializes in ensuring families have adequate protection for health and life as well as insuring people with histories of cancer and other major illnesses.

Mr. Davis comes from a family of five siblings and was raised in Jim Crow Era Birmingham, Alabama in a mixed race family. A survivor of the 15 September 1963 church bombing that took the lives of the four little girls at Sixteenth Street Baptist Church, he has long been a fighter for human and civil rights. His mother would take him to see Ralph Abernathy and Martin Luther King speak at his church; ultimately leading to the bombing of his Sunday school class by the KKK.

Following the murder of his father in 1968, Mr. Davis has devoted his life to standing for human rights and social justice. He has filmed documentaries in New Orleans following the aftermath of Hurricane Katrina covering human rights violations. In May of 2010 he filmed the survivors and descendents of prisoners of the internment camp at Ft. Lincoln, North Dakota – documenting the abuse of German and Japanese American Citizens during

World War II. He has also filmed in Alaska and covered stories on systematic parental alienation by the courts and violations of men's rights. In 1996 he founded the Community Coalition, an organization focused on human rights using media campaigns to inform the public. His television shows focus on positive people in the community. He covers risky stories that main stream media will not touch. He began broadcasting in 2004 with the first purchase of an Internet TV channel and his cable TV programming began in 2007.

Mr. Davis has degrees in Nautical Industrial Technology and Information Technology with an advanced Information Systems Technology Certification. He is a certified Chemical Dependency Treatment Specialist and a graduate of the Navy Drug and Alcohol Counselor Program.

Walter's bio written by Art Kirsch for http://socalshowbiz.com. For the complete article: http://socalshowbiz.com/people-in-the-spotlight/115-spotlight-on-walter-davis

CHAPTER 1

Sudanese Marriage

$\wp$

What is Marriage?

Historical Definition

Marriage is the formal union of a man and a woman, typically recognized by law, by which they become husband and wife. Marriage is uniquely beneficial to society because it is the foundation of the family and the basic building block of society.

• It brings significant stability and meaning to human relationships.

• It is the ideal environment for the raising of children.

• It plays an important role in transmitting culture and civilization to future generations.

Marriage is not merely a private contract, but a social institution of great public value and concern. Although the institution of marriage pre-dates reliable recorded history, many cultures have legends concerning the origins of marriage. The way in which a marriage is conducted and its rules and ramifications have changed over time. The institution itself, depending on the culture or demographic of the time has changed. Various cultures have had their own theories on the origin of marriage. One example may lie in a man's need for assurance as to paternity of his children.

He might therefore be willing to pay a bride price or provide for a woman in exchange for exclusive sexual access. Legitimacy is the consequence of this transaction rather than its motivation.

Biblical Definition

Biblically, marriage is in balance, with Christ as the head of the man and the wife together. The biblical concept described marriage as oneness between two individuals that pictures the oneness of Christ with His church. The creation of marriage is recorded in Genesis (2:23-24): The man said, "this is now bone of my bones and flesh of my flesh; she shall be called woman, for she was taken out of man." For this reason a man will leave his father and mother and be united to his wife, and they will become one flesh. God created man and then made woman to complement him. Marriage is God's "fix" for the fact that it is not good for the man to be alone (Genesis 2:18).

Sudanese Cultural Perspective

Marriage is one of the most important Sudanese traditions, and is arranged by the families of the bride and groom. Divorce among the Sudanese is not unheard of; it is usually caused by a lack of children. If a woman does not produce children, a man can demand the return of the cattle he paid for the marriage and can send the woman back to her own village. Marriage takes place in stages, however. A marriage is not finalized until the bride has given birth to at least two or more children. When a third child is born, the marriage is considered "tied." At this point, the wife and the children become full members of the husband's clan. Women desire to have more children. A man may have multiple wives, who do not necessarily live close to each other. But they will all live in the same compound of the husband's land. In Sudan, man is the head of the household and speaks for the family.

Marriage customs vary depending on tribal traditions. In South Sudanese communities children are encouraged to stay with their parents until they are married or mature and economically independent enough to live on their own. Marriage in many South Sudanese communities is a social affair, which may involve many members of the extended family. Among some tribes, especially Nuer and Dinka, the approval of the maternal uncle is essential. Marriage in Sudanese culture means stability.

A man or a woman who is not married is considered not stable. Children are a savings account to the family; therefore, they are raised to service their families in turn when they grow up. A girl brings wealth to the family when she gets married because the husband pays a dowry. This dowry is usually 25-50 cows and money that is equivalent to the number of cows in Nuer. This total goes up to 100 cows in Dinka. A boy is a foundation and a protector of the family. Some other tribes in South Sudan pay less in marriage in comparison to Nuer and Dinka. By looking at this traditional Sudanese aspect of marriage, it would make sense if one viewed this as business. Indeed, it's a business to me.

A man marries more wives with hope to produce more children, to gain wealth and prestige in the society. The more boys a man has, the more powerful he will be when these boys become men. When one looks at the definition of marriage, in comparison to the Sudanese culture, it becomes no longer a marriage between "A man and a woman" because it is no longer between the two, but a man and women. This is unconventional; therefore, it does not fit into the biblical definition of marriage.

Some societies are flexible in allowing other types of unconventional marriage arrangements. Nuer tribes of South Sudan are an example. A woman who is unable to have children is sometimes married as a "husband" to another woman who then is impregnated by a secret boyfriend. The barren woman becomes the socially recognized father and thereby adds members to her father's patrilineal kin group.

The Nuer also has several forms of "spiritual marriage." A man may marry a woman as a stand-in for his deceased brother. The children that are born of this union will be considered descendants of the dead man; therefore, the "spirit" is the socially recognized father. This allows the continuation of his family line and succession to an important social position. Married Nuer women traditionally have no significant wealth; it belongs to their husbands. With this form of "spiritual marriage," there will be no living husband, though she may subsequently have children. She is, in effect, a widow who takes care of her husband's wealth and children until they are mature (Zeitzen, 2008).

Spiritual marriage is a traditional type of marriage developed by the Nuer tribe of the South Sudan to continue lineage under atypical circumstances. The Nuer are strongly patrilineal. They believe that males must carry on the family name with male heirs. Spiritual marriage developed as a way to counter-act the occurrence of a married male dying before he was able to produce many sons. The mother of the household would be expected to take a husband with whom she would produce heirs in the name of her deceased husband. This man would be chosen from her husband's lineage, such as her husband's brother or a son from another marriage, and he would be expected to impregnate the dead man's wife to produce more children.

This "spiritual husband" would be considered the deceased husband until his duty of producing many children for his deceased kinsman was fulfilled. The "uncle" would only then be able to start his own family. This way, men end up with wives even though many are not technically considered to be real wives. All Nuer men are expected to have sons and prefer to have their own children; however, they consider mystical explanations to justify spiritual marriages. In many senses, Nuer believe that a dead man or a barren woman can indeed curse the family. In order to make the dead man happy, the family members have to marry a woman for him or keep his family line going. Barren women usually marry while they are alive, so they can choose who they want among their relatives to bear children for them.

Nuer women should never desert their deceased husbands, but sometimes the women will live in a home specified for widows. This can occur before or even during the "spiritual marriage". Basically, this means that the women do not have to live with their "new" husband. If the widow is still in her child bearing years, it is the husband's brother's duty to provide for the family. The children will still be considered the deceased husband's and not the brother's. The woman does not need to have a wedding ceremony with the dead husband's brother. She is already regarded as his wife. Spiritual marriage is also seen when a wealthy and powerful Nuer woman maintains an already deceased male as her husband. This is the result of an attempt to keep her wealth to herself instead of marrying a living man which would ensure that he would control her resources. In this situation, children still inherit the name of the dead husband but additionally receive the property of their mother.

Two main beliefs among the Nuer regarding spiritual marriage include a strong loyalty to the fallen kinsman without a son. There is a belief that the deceased would rise up against his lineage and cause misfortune for them if no son was produced in his name. This custom ensures that the family will be protected from illness and any other tragedy that could and often does occur. Another form of spiritual marriage used by the Nuer is the levirate. The heir to the deceased male inherits assets and liabilities in addition to his wife or wives. He is still expected to act as his deceased kinsman would. This ensures that the dead man's wealth and assets remain within his own family.

The Nuer carried on the custom of spiritual marriage for many reasons. It is not only plays an important role in the kinship system, but also assists in maintaining social control among this egalitarian society. Without this unique custom, it would be difficult to trace relatives. The population of the tribe would not be able to stabilize itself. In addition to spiritual marriage, Zeitzen (2008) thinks the Nuer practice "blind-eye" adultery and woman-to-woman marriage that assist a woman who cannot bear a child, continuing on the patrilineal kinship system. This is no different from the Western practice of unconventional marriage called "homosexual or lesbian marriage" except the Sudanese do it under one condition: the barren woman does not do anything sexually to her wife. The Nuer's barren woman provides for her wife as a man; she works outside as a bread winner, while her wife does the household shores. The barren woman becomes the identified husband, so she cannot cook, clean up, or tend the children unless she wants to help as a husband.

Family Characteristics

The traditional Sudanese family orientation is hierarchical with an extended family that provides support. Families have strong religious orientation and strong family kinship. Authority rests with the males, the elders, and parents. Sue and Sue (1990) quoted in Gashaw-Gant (2004) describe such a traditional orientation:

> Within the family, the father assumes the role of the primary authority figure. Children are seen as a source of income. They are expected to be obedient and are usually not consulted on family decisions. The sexual behaviors of adolescent females are severely restricted and sexual topics are rarely discussed with children. Children are expected to contribute financially to the family when possible. Parents reciprocate by providing for them though young adulthood and even after marriage (abin. p. 232-233).

In Sudanese culture, older children are expected to take responsibility for household chores such as cleaning, cooking, tending to younger siblings, and herding livestock at an early age. For adolescents to enter into marriage and parenthood during early life is not uncommon. They perceive marriage as a stabilizing influence. Marriage is highly valued: it is viewed as the foundation of a strong society. On the other hand, in both the Christian and Islamic religions, marriage has a different perspective. Girls are allowed to marry at a younger age than their counterparts in the United States.

Within the Islamic religion, marriage is allowed between relatives. According to Teebi and Rabah (1999) quoted in Gashaw-Gant (2004), in the Islamic religion marriage between cousins is socially acceptable. In the Islamic faith, having more than one wife is also allowed. Harmony between these wives is encouraged. Outside the extended family unit, men and women do not typically interact socially. In general, religion teaches against or forbids divorce.

Further, family relationships within these cultures can be seen as sources of support through both good and bad times. Families are expected to stay together and to share all aspects of challenges. Traditional families are hierarchical in structure, with special attention given to elders who are seen as a source of wisdom. Filial respect is given at all times. In the United States, refugee/immigrant families from this community are faced with overwhelming challenges in trying to keep their families together (Gashaw-Gant, 2004).

Nuer Historical Facts

The Nuer, also known as the Nei Ti Naath, roughly meaning original people, and are a confederation of tribes located in South Sudan and western Ethiopia. Collectively, the Nuer form one of the largest ethnic groups in East Africa. They are a pastoral people who rely on cattle products and farms for almost every aspect of their daily lives. The Nuer border such tribes as the Dinka, Murle, Shilluk, Chay, and Anyuak.

The Nuer are among the very few African tribes that successfully fended off colonial powers in the early 20th century. The Zulu tribes of South Africa were similar in this aspect. The Nuer warriors are among the most skilled fighters in Africa. They wielded spears, mut or bith, made of finely crafted iron. The nature of relations among these various South Sudanese tribes was greatly affected in the 19th century by the intrusion of Ottomans, Arabs, and eventually the British. Some ethnic groups made their accommodation with the imperial attackers and others did not, in effect pitting one South ethnic group against another in the context of foreign rule. For example, some sections of the Dinka and other South Sudanese tribes were more accommodating to British rule than were the Nuer (Evan-Pritchard, 1948). The Nuer of the Anglo-Egyptian Sudan were the last indigenous people in British Africa to be conquered by force of arms (Evans-Pritchard, 1951). Therefore, in my opinion, the British prevented the cultivation of fruit-bearing trees, such as mangos and other related fruit trees in Nuer land as a punishment for their resistance to Britain's rule.

Because Nuer were furious in fighting the colonial government, the Dinka treated the resisting Nuer as hostile, so hostility developed between the two groups as a result of their differing relationships with the British. This has been documented by Douglas Johnson (1994) in his book "Nuer Prophets." In 2006, the Nuer were also the tribe in South Sudan, which resisted disarming most strongly. The Lou Nuer, a subgroup of Nuer, most strongly resisted the Sudan Peoples Liberation Army or SPLA disarmament campaign. This was chiefly because the government failed to provide adequate security to guard them from aggressors, such as the Murle. They refused to lay down their weapons which led to SPLA soldiers confiscating Nuer cattle and destroying their economy. The authorities later refused to compensate them.

Nuer Culture

Nuer culture has been closely identified with cattle. This has been documented by early researchers in the Nuer land, such as Evan-Pritchard (1948-51); Johnson (1994-97) and Hutchinson (1951). Cattle have historically been of the highest symbolic religious and economic value among the Nuer. Cattle are particularly important in their role as bride wealth, where they are given by a husband's lineage to his wife's lineage. It is this exchange of cattle which ensures that the children will be considered members of the husband's lineage and part of his line of descent. The classical Nuer institution of spiritual marriage, in which a man can "father" children after his death, is based on this practice of cattle exchanges to define relations of kinship and descent.

In their turn, cattle given over to the wife's patrilineage enable the male children of that patrilineage to marry, and thereby ensure the continuity of her patrilineage. We have learned previously in this chapter, barren women can even take wives of their own, whose children, obviously biologically fathered by men from outside unions, then become members of her patrilineage and she is legally and culturally their father, allowing her to participate in reproduction in a metaphorical sense. Evans-Pritchard (1948) studied the Nuer and made very detailed accounts of his interactions. Anthropologists, such Evans-Pritchard (1948) and Sharon Hutchinson (1951) have done intensive research in Nuer land.

This research produced the very first book published about this culture. Evans-Pritchard also describes Nuer cosmology and religion in his books. This set the stage for the new South Sudanese researchers to come.

In the 1990s, Sharon Hutchinson (1951) returned to Nuerland to update Evans-Pritchard's account. She found that the Nuer had placed strict limits on the convertibility of money and cattle in order to preserve the special status of cattle as objects of bride wealth exchange and as mediators to the divine. She also found that as a result of endemic warfare with the Sudanese state, guns had acquired much of the symbolic and ritual importance previously held by cattle.

Nuer tradition has been the same, in terms of language and norms across Nuer land, from Bentiu to far eastern Nuer bordered by Ethiopia. The people speak the Nuer language which belongs to the Nilo-Saharan language phylum. The Nuer receive facial markings called "gaar" as part of their initiation into adulthood. The pattern of Nuer scarification varies within specific subgroups. The most common initiation pattern among males consists of six parallel horizontal lines which are cut across the forehead with a razor, often with a dip in the lines above the nose. Dotted or "bieer" patterns are also common, especially among the Nuer of Bentiu, "Bul Nuer" and among females as a part of beauty.

These have been practiced across Nuer land for decades. However, this Nuer traditional marking is slowly diminishing as their typical culture is being diluted by the western culture and surrounding east African neighboring countries' cultures. Typical foods eaten by the Nuer tribe include beef, goat, cow's milk, mangos, and sorghum in one of three forms: "kop" finely ground, handled until balled and boiled, "wal wal or nup" ground, lightly balled and boiled to a solid porridge, and yot-yot, similar to Ethiopian's injera.

Because of the civil wars in South Sudan over the past 50 years, many Nuer have emmigrated to Kenya, Ethiopia and elsewhere. Approximately 80,000 Nuer were resettled in the United States as refugees since the early 1990s. Many Nuer are now residing in Nebraska, Minnesota, Sag Harbor, NY, Iowa, South Dakota, Tennessee, Georgia, California, Utah, Arizona, Texas, and many other states. Some of them are living in Canada; the majority live in Toronto, Kitchener, Edmonton, and Calgary. There are currently over 20,000 South Sudanese in Australia. Perhaps a third of this number is Nuer (Ferraro, 2008).

1.   Merriam Webster's Collegiate Dictionary (2002). Merriam -Webster, Incorporated (10th ed). Springfield, Massachussets, U.S.A.
2.   Bell, D. (1997). Defining of marriage and legitimacy. Current Anthropology, 38 (2) 237–254
3.   Gough, E. K. (1959). The nayars and the definition of marriage. Royal Anthropological Institute of Great Britain and Ireland, 89, 23-34.

CHAPTER 2

Guiding Teenagers in Marriage Partner Selection

ॐ

Almost this entire chapter has been adapted with recognition and full credit given to the Secret of Family Happiness (1996) due to its similarity to the way the South Sudanese approach their marriage. According to the secret of family happiness (1996), selecting a marriage partner is very much a culturally defined process. The rules governing selection vary widely from society to society and are often complex.

• How would you go about selecting a long-term mate?

• Where would you begin?

• What criteria would you use?

• Would you take the views and wishes of your relatives and friends into consideration?

When we look around the world to see how other societies deal with these questions, it is clear that love and sexual compatibility are not always the basis for selecting a spouse. However, when romantic love is an important criterion, physical beauty is frequently a key factor. Age, health, body shape, and especially facial appearance are usually the focus. What is considered to be attractive varies considerably from culture to culture. It is clear that

concepts of beauty are not universal. Some traditional societies of
Africa, such as Nuer tribe in South Sudan and the South Pacific,
define large, plump bodies as being attractive, especially for
women. Nuer preferred large ladies for three reasons: they want
a woman who is going to give birth to big men (the Nuer would
call this lady, Man Dhooli or mother of boys), a woman who is
going to produce quality and quantity productivities, and a lady
who will not be easily harmed during starvation. Europeans and
North Americans today usually define such a body shape as being
unhealthy and even ugly; however, ideals of beauty change over
time.

What to Look for in a Mate

Is it customary where you live for a person to choose his or her own
marriage mate? If so, how should you proceed if you find someone
of the opposite sex attractive? First, ask yourself whether marriage
really is my intention. It is cruel to play with another person's
emotions by raising false expectations. Then ask yourself, am I in a
position to get married? If the answer to both questions is positive,
the steps you take next will vary depending on local custom. In
some cultures, after observing for a while, you might approach the
person and express a desire to get better acquainted. If the response
is negative, do not persist to the point of being objectionable.

Remember, the other person also has a right to make a decision in
the matter. If, however, the response is positive, you may arrange to
spend time together in wholesome activities. This will give you an
opportunity to see whether marriage to this person would be wise.
Research has documented that it is important for both prospects
to have common beliefs and principles. The Secret of Family
Happiness (1996) illustrates this. It is more likely that there will be
severe disharmony if marriage occurs between two people who do

not share the same beliefs and faith. On the other hand, a mutual devotion to whatever faith that both of you have is the strongest basis for unity. While sharing a common philosophical view in many areas, define and clarify your goals. Define how you both feel about having children or what things have priority in your life. In truly successful marriages, the couples are good friends and enjoy each other's company. Thus, they need to have interests in common.

It is difficult to sustain a close friendship, much less a marriage, when this is not the case. Still, if your prospective partner enjoys a particular activity, such as going to movies every week, and you do not, does that mean that the two of you should not get married? Not necessarily. Perhaps you share other, more important interests. Moreover, you might give happiness to your prospective partner by sharing in wholesome activities because the other person enjoys them. In Nuer one of the most important issues to be considered by both prospective partners is having the same religion. This is not always the case, but it is important that both of you consider the ramifications of being Christian, Muslim, or other religions.

Indeed, to a large degree, compatibility is determined by how adaptable both of you are rather than by how identical you are. Instead of asking, "Do we agree on everything?", a better question might be "What happens when we disagree?"; "Can we discuss matters calmly, while maintaining respect and dignity for each other?" Or do discussions often deteriorate into heated arguments? If you want to get married, be wary of anyone who is proud and opinionated, never willing to compromise or who constantly demands and schemes to have his or her own way.

What to Learn in Advance

• Within the process of getting to know each other, a woman has to ask, what kind of reputation does this man have?

• Who are his friends?

• Does he display self-control?

• How does he treat elderly people?

• Does he abuse alcoholic beverages?

Also:

• What kind of family does he come from?

• How does he interact with his family?

• What is his attitude toward money?

These are all necessary in this modern life, but are not obstacles in the South Sudanese tradition.

A man may ask:

• Does this woman display love and respect?

• Is she capable of caring for a home?

• What will her family expect of us?

• Is she wise, industrious, thrifty, trustworthy?

• What does she talk about?

• Is she genuinely concerned about the welfare of others, or is she self-centered?

• Is she willing to submit to headship, or is she stubborn, perhaps even rebellious?

I want you to keep in mind that if you have a relationship with someone about whom you have serious reservations, it is wise to discontinue the relationship and to refrain from making a lasting commitment to that person.

Keep Your Courtship Honorable

Sexual acts have never been part of the South Sudanese traditional dating ritual. A man shows how gentle and trusted he is so that a girl should trust him. Sexual acts during the dating ritual demonstrates key issues about both of these prospective lovers; both male and female can sit at close proximity avoiding inappropriate touching. If any of them arched by sexual feeling, it shows how lighthearted this individual is. Nobody wants to be termed lighthearted because is a bad character in marriage. Nobody wants to marry a lighthearted man or a woman who will bring you problems later.

How can you keep your courtship honorable? First, make sure that your moral conduct is above reproach. Where you live, is holding hands, kissing, or embracing considered appropriate behavior for unmarried couples? Even if such expression of affection is not frowned upon, they should be allowed only when the relationship has reached a point where marriage is definitely planned. Be careful that displays of affection do not escalate into unclean conduct or even fornication.

Because the heart is treacherous, both of you would be wise to avoid being isolated in a house, an apartment, a parked automobile, or anywhere else that would give opportunity for wrong conduct. Keeping your courtship moral and clean gives clear evidence that you have self-control and that you put unselfish concern for the other person's welfare ahead of your own desires. Honorable courtship also includes honest communication. As your courtship progresses toward marriage, certain matters will need to be discussed openly. These are the matters to consider: where will you live? Will both of you work? Do you want to have children?

In this modern life, the world has become global village; therefore the traditional way of life has changed. It is absolutely fair to reveal things, perhaps in one's past, that could affect the marriage. These many include major debts or obligations or health matters, such as any serious disease or condition you may have. Since many persons who are infected with HIV (the virus that cause AIDS) show no immediate symptoms, it would not be wrong for an individual or for caring parents to request an AIDS blood test of one who has in the past engaged in sexual promiscuity or was an intravenous drug user. If the test proves positive, the infected person should not pressure the intended mate to continue the relationship if that one now wishes to terminate it. Really, anyone who has engaged in a high-risk life-style would do well to submit voluntarily to an AIDS blood test before beginning a courtship.

Looking Beyond The Wedding

In South Sudan, a newly married couple would stay with the groom's parents until they are able to manage their family. Both would get support from the bride and groom's family. During the final months before the marriage, both partners will likely be very busy with arranging for the wedding. You can alleviate much of the tension by being moderate. An elaborate wedding may please relatives and the community, but it may leave newlyweds and their families physically exhausted and drained. While adherence to local customs is reasonable, lavish and competitive conformity can overshadow the meaning of the occasion. This robs some couples of the joy that is possible.

The feelings of others must be considered. The groom is primarily responsible for deciding what will go on at the wedding. It is important for couples to remember that the wedding is just one day. Marriage lasts a lifetime. Couples should avoid concentrating too much on the act of getting married. Instead, they should look to their faith for guidance. Marriage requires planning ahead for life. A successful marriage requires preparation.

Universal Factors for a Lasting Marriage

According to the Secret of Family Happiness (1996), there are vital factors required for a long lasting marriage. If both the husband and the wife put these to use, they will unlock the door to happiness and many blessings. What are these?

The first key is love. The Christian Bible identifies different kinds of love. One is a warm, personal affection for someone, the kind of love that exists between close friends (John 11:3). Another is the love that grows between family members (Romans 12:10). A third is the romantic love that one can have for a member of the opposite sex. All these should be cultivated for a husband and wife.

Another factor is respect. When married people really love each other, they will also have respect for each other. Respect is a vital factor to a happy marriage. Respect is defined as giving consideration to others and honoring them. To enjoy a happy marriage, one must be concerned for the interests of their partner as well as their own. If one only considers what is good for themselves, this could be interpreted as selfish. The priorities of the relationship have to come first. Mutual respect is integral to help couples acknowledge and manage differences in viewpoint. It is not reasonable to expect two people to have identical views on everything. What may be important to a husband may not be as important to a wife. What a wife likes may not be what a husband likes. Each should respect the views and choices of the other, as long as they are married. Sharing household chores, finances, and tending of the children is part of showing respect to one another.

Preparing for a Successful Marriage

Preparing for a successful marriage is not easy. Preparing for a successful marriage is similar to preparing the design of a tall building. It must be prepared to resist earth quakes and other disasters. A building has to have a strong foundation just as a successful marriage does. What are the steps to consider when contemplating marriage? There are three steps to consider:

• How can a person tell whether he or she is ready for marriage?

• What should be looked for in a mate?

• How can courtship be kept honorable?

Using the same scenario, constructing a building may be expensive, but caring for its long-term maintenance is costly as well. It is similar with marriage. Getting married seems challenging enough; however, maintaining a marital relationship year after year must also be considered. One may ask a question, what does maintaining such as relationship entail? A vital factor is a wholehearted commitment. If one is contemplating marriage, the secret of family happiness (1996) suggests you bear a wholehearted commitment, knowing that the two will stay together for life. The idea of a life time commitment frightens many prospective couples, but if you really love the person you intend to marry, commitment will not seem like a burden. Instead, it will be viewed as a source of security.

The sense of commitment implied in marriage will make a couple want to stay together through good and bad times and to be supportive of each other. Maturity is an important factor. Some people should wait until they are past the bloom of youth. In this period sexual feelings run strong and can distort one's judgment. It is true that young people change rapidly as they grow up. Many who marry when very young find that after just a few years their needs and desires, as well as those of their mate, have changed. Statistics reveal that teenagers who marry are much more likely to be unhappy and seek divorce than those who wait a little longer.

Do not rush into marriage. Some years spent living as a young, single adult can help develop maturity. This may result in being a better qualified and suitable mate. Waiting to get married can also help you to understand yourself better. This is necessary if you are to develop a successful relationship in your marriage.

Know Yourself First

Do you find it easy to list the qualities you want in a mate? Most people do. However, what about your own qualities? What traits do you have that will help you contribute to a successful marriage? What type of husband or wife will you be? For example, do you freely admit your mistakes and accept advice, or are you always defensive when corrected? Are you generally cheerful and optimistic, or do you tend to be gloomy, frequently complaining? Remember, marriage will not change your personality. If you are proud, oversensitive, or overly pessimistic when single, you will be the same when married. Since it is difficult to see ourselves the way others see us, why not ask a parent or a trusted friend for frank comments and suggestions? If you learn of changes that could be made, work on these before taking steps to marry.

Trial or Cohabitation Marriage

Many couples claim that living together before marriage will help them test out their compatibility. Trial marriage does not test one of the most crucial elements of marriage: commitment. One thing to keep in mind: a domineering attitude will lead to trouble in a marriage.

Marriage of References

Many societies have specific kinds of second marriage rules that anthropologists refer to as the levirate and the sororate. The levirate specifies that a widow should marry the brother of her deceased husband. The rationale for this rule is that it keeps the dead man's children and wealth within his family. It also maintains the existing bond between the two families. The levirate was named after Levi the son of Jacob in the Judeo-Christian Old Testament. It is a marriage rule that was common in Jewish society several thousand years ago and in other patrilineal societies that have polygyny (Carisle, 1990).

Multicultural Perspective on Marriage

The marriage process often involves a predetermined agreement to transfer wealth or to perform labor for one's in-laws. In the mostly monogamous societies of Europe and Asia, this traditionally has been in the form of a dowry, which is money or property given by the bride's family to the groom, ostensibly to establish a new household or estate (Ember & Melvin, 1998). It is, in a sense, the bride's share of the family inheritance. Dowries may be intensely negotiated, especially when the bride's family is wealthy. Until the early 20th century in Europe, rich families commonly hired lawyers do draw up formal marriage contracts that often specified the dowry details. The North American traditions of the "hope chest" and the bride's family paying for the wedding are survivors of a dowry system (Ferraro, 2008).

In India today, the failure to pay all of an agreed upon dowry amount is considered an extremely serious problem. It places a newly married young woman in a difficult and dangerous position in the home that she shares with her husband's family. Hundreds of these brides die each year in what are euphemistically referred to as "kitchen accidents" (Ferraro, 2008). In fact, some are killed by the husband, mother-in-law, or other members of his family who view the failure to pay the agreed upon dowry as being a breach of contract and the ruining of his life. The death of his "failed" wife allows him to marry again and to obtain the dowry that his family believes he deserves.

Bride Price is the reverse of a dowry. It involves the groom giving things of high value to the bride's father. Bride Price is most common among polygynous, small-scale, patrilineal societies-- especially in sub-Saharan Africa and among Native Americans (O'Neal, 2008). When European missionaries first encountered Bride Price, they misinterpreted it as being nothing more than a demeaning "bride purchase." It actually is a way of showing respect for the bride and her parents. At the same time, it is a compensation for the bride's family for the loss of her economic services. It is very important to understand that it is also a way of validating the groom's right to future offspring. In some societies, children are not "legitimate" if their father did not pay a Bride Price. It is more important than a marriage ceremony in establishing legitimacy.

More often, the Bride Price is large enough to require kinsmen to help the groom in making the payment. Nuer people of South Sudan are still holding onto this tradition. It is especially common among pastoralists' societies, such as the cattle herders of East Africa who have traditionally paid Bride Price with cows. Among tribes, such as Nuer of South Sudan, Turkana, and Masai of Kenya, borrowing to make up the agreed upon Bride Price puts the groom in debt to his older male relatives for many years (O'Neal, 2008). The bride's father usually disburses the payment in turn as Bride Price for his sons and nephews. As a result, the community's wealth is circulated among relatives and close friends.

Among these tribes, the bride's family has a strong economic interest in keeping her marriage together because a divorce would require the return of the Bride Price, which often has already been given away to relatives. If there are children, however, the Bride Price usually does not have to be returned, but the children belong to the groom's family. He keeps the children instead of the Bride Price. In a sense, the Bride Price becomes a payment for children and, therefore, has also been referred to as "progeny price" or a genetic descendant's right as a shareholder.

In societies with little material wealth and social rules requiring sharing, it is rarely possible to accumulate a Bride Price. This is sometimes a give and take situation rather than entitlement in the Nuer culture. Those who do not have sisters or daughters to pay back their relatives sometimes are asked to return those cows, especially when their relationship goes wrong. As a result, such societies often have Bride Service instead. In some cultures, when a groom does not have enough to pay, he would agree to work for his in-laws for a set period of time. Among the Yanomamö and other lowland forest peoples of South America, this service may go on for years. Making it more difficult is the fact that Yanomamö men are customarily prevented from speaking directly to their in-laws and must avoid them (Zeitzen, 2008).

In Melanesia, the Amazon Basin of South America, and scattered elsewhere among warlike peoples, there have been cultural patterns allowing marriage by capture as an alternative method of acquiring a wife (Zeitzen, 2008). It has occurred usually when bride price could not be arranged or when women were in short supply. It is a mistake to assume that marriage by capture is always a forceful act on an unwilling woman.

At times, it is merely a ritual or a cover for a prearranged elopement, which also has been a revolutionary Nuer's way of marriage as a result of the civil war. Many individuals Nuer men cannot afford to pay up to the maximum bride price anymore; therefore, the easiest way of marriage has been through the elopement process. Many Nuer men who have married through elopement are now returning home from exile to the new country to complete their wedding obligations; otherwise, they have no legitimate wives in the eyes of the Nuer customary laws.

In contemporary Japan there is a system of traditional gift exchanges between the groom's and the bride's families that does not neatly fit the usual definition of a dowry or a bride price as several tribes of South Sudan, especially the Nuer and the Dinka, have been practicing for decades. They have essentially combined both patterns in a largely symbolic gift exchange. When a couple becomes engaged, the two sets of parents formally exchange betrothal or a mutual promise gifts with each other, thereby reinforcing that the marriage will be a bond between the families rather than just the young couple.

In the Tokyo region, these "yuino" gifts usually consist of nine items that are considered to be auspicious, e.g., abalone, dried bonito, dried kelp, etc. (Zeitzen, 2008). During this ceremony, the groom also gives "yuinokin" betrothal money to his future bride's family. It is understood that this money is to be used in establishing a household for the newlywed couple. In South Sudanese culture, especially Nuer tribe of the South Sudan, newlywed couples often stay with the groom's parents until they gain property to maintain their independence. During the late 1990's this betrothal money averaged 878,000 yen in Japan, a little more than $7,300 U.S. dollars at the time (Zeitzen, 2008). It is popular for urban Japanese couples to design their own wedding rituals and to incorporate North American traditions, e.g., white wedding dresses, tiered wedding cakes, etc. It is also very popular to get married in Hawaii and other places outside of Japan. South Sudanese have adapted the same marriage rituals, with white wedding dresses, kissing, tiered wedding cakes, and honeymoon.

Divorce Rate Statistics

Sudanese are community oriented people. Marriages are traditionally arranged by the parents of the couple. This is still the case today, even among wealthier and more educated Sudanese. In Muslim groups of Sudan, matches are often made between cousins, second cousins, or other family members, or if not, at least between members of the same tribe and social class (Ember & Melvin, 1998). Parents conduct the negotiations and it is common for a bride and groom not to have seen each other before the wedding. Significant age differences between husband and wife are not uncommon. Extended families often live together under the same roof, or at least nearby. With all these cultural values the Sudanese have, it is appropriate for a couple to want to invite their parents into therapy sessions. In South Sudan, marriage or dissolving a marriage is the responsibility of both parents of the couple.

Marriage and divorce are both have common experiences in any culture, but in Western cultures, more than 90 percent of people marry by age 50. Healthy marriages are good for couples' mental and physical health. They are also good for children. Research reveals that growing up in a happy home protects children from mental, physical, educational and social problems (Baker, 2007). However, about 40 to 50 percent of married couples in the United States divorce. The divorce rate for subsequent marriages is even higher.

The chart below illustrates the average age at marriage and a breakdown in percentages for men and women who divorce in America

Age	Women	Men
Under 20 years old	27.6%	11.7%
20 to 24 years old	36.6%	38.8%
25 to 29 years old	16.4%	22.3%
30 to 34 years old	8.5%	11.6%
35 to 39 years old	5.1%	6.5%

The divorce rate in America for first marriage, vs. second or third marriage: 50% percent of first marriages, 67% of second and 74% of third marriages end in divorce, according to Jennifer Baker of the Forest Institute of Professional Psychology in Springfield, Missouri (2007). According to enrichment journal (2009) on the divorce rate in America:

1. The divorce rate in America for first marriage is 41%
2. The divorce rate in America for second marriage is 60%
3. The divorce rate in America for third marriage is 73%

According to the Discovery Channel, couples with children have a slightly lower rate of divorce than childless couples. Sociologists believe that childlessness is also a common cause of divorce. The absence of children leads to loneliness and weariness. In the United States at least 66 per cent of all divorced couples are childless. This is also the case in the South Sudanese community worldwide. The divorce rate increased dramatically because familial support is no longer a safety net for many members of the young generation outside and inside South Sudan.

CHAPTER 3

Sudanese Cultural Crisis in the West

ℰↃ

What is going on in the Sudanese families in the West? In the 1990s, a large number of Sudanese refugees arrived in the United States with hoping to settle and rest after a decades of civil war in Sudan. They arrived with high expectations and hopes to provide food and shelter for their families here as well as back home in Sudan. Both men and women joined the workforce to provide for their families; therefore, the power in the family no longer resides solely with men.

Women are no longer the domestic workers only; they are the providers as well. Women expect their husbands to help them with duties in the house, but men often under mind this change and resist helping their wives with domestic chores. They resist assisting their wives with cooking, cleaning, giving baths to children, baby-sitting, and cleaning bathrooms. With this imbalance of duties in the family, women often become frustrated and demonstrate extreme anger toward men. Men feel they have lost their manly controlling power they used to have in Sudan when women exercise their claim to equality.

There is a power struggle between South Sudanese men and women in the west. Women have become more powerful because the laws protect victims of physical and emotional abuse. Perpetrators are prosecuted in the west.

When a family dispute erupts out of control, physical fighting is more likely between a husband and wife. The wife in many cases is the one who initiates a 911emergency call for police assistance. When a police officer shows up, someone in that family must go to jail. Often perpetrators are men who did not understand they live in a culture that does not allow their traditional way of disciplining with physical violence. After serving time in jail, this man may not return back home. South Sudanese men go through a lot before joining the family again. Even if a man returns back to the family, the relationship may never be the same again. Differences may always exist and the solution could lead to separation.

In some cases, law enforcement agencies do not realize that their intervention is doing more harm than good to Sudanese families. During incarceration men are separated from their families and leave the wives and children at home without support. Often men lose the respect of their families and no longer have influence over their spouses. They lose self-respect and the respect of their families. They lose the power of decision making. For the first time in the Sudanese tradition, separation has become a common solution to the family dispute, with men being kicked out of their homes. About 90% of separations reach complete divorce within six to nine months.

In this cultural war, women usually keep the children and men become victims of child support enforcement. This results in disruption of the tradition of the man keeping the children. This results in disruption of the extended family as the traditional arena for family dispute resolution with external forces assuming the role traditionally exercised by elder family members.

Family Crisis Explored

Women may feel victorious for successfully eliminating the abuser in their life and become free in their opinions, but another problem occurs shortly after that. In all cases, the welfare of the children and future challenges on the single parent are usually overlooked.

Within these six to nine months after separation of the parents, the mother might select a boyfriend in some cases kicked out by his wife. When this relationship is noticed by the children, another war occurs again between the mother and her children. The children may react by expressing anger, depression and disrespect to their mother as a result of the affair. They may start being truant more often and finally drop out of school completely. When this occurs, children are more likely to use alcohol and or other drugs, and finally run away from home.

Many teens end up with pregnancies out of wedlock. Even in a normal Sudanese home, where separation or divorce is not a problem, parents and children represent two different cultures, Western and Sudanese. While parents tend to observe traditional South Sudanese traditions, their children embrace western ways overall. Parents often want their children to behave and obey their rules, while children often ignore these demands and perceive their parents as idiots due to the fact that the majority of parents do not know how to read and write in the English language as well as their own dialects.

Children see themselves in a superior position and often undermine their family's rules. On the other hand, parents tend to view their children as rebellious and lost. Positive communication is out of the question; therefore, parents and their children become isolated from one another. This is what South Sudanese families are often experiencing in the Western world.

Over-Arching Issues in the South Sudanese Community

An over-arching issue is the loss of faith and cultural values, which guided this population for decades. Being an insider of this community, I have witnessed issues that are fundamental obstacles for growth for newly resettled refugees and immigrants in the United States. Due to the diaspora of this community, these issues also exist now within South Sudan. The problem in this community has been a lack of understanding of the leadership function.

While ignorance is widespread, a majority pretend to understand the dynamics of the leadership situation. There is a failure to understand that leaders come and go, but the community remains for generations to come. The leadership struggle is a virus that affects South Sudanese families locally, nationally and abroad. What am I referring to? There is a leadership division along tribal lines within South Sudanese communities throughout the United States. Non-profit community centers have been established along tribal lines, either Nuer dominating or Dinka dominating. This division is not only in the community based organizations, but also in the South Sudanese churches. When it comes to each tribal establishment, sub-division occurs and becomes an internal problem for that particular tribe.

The Nuer community in particular has its issues. Nuer people in the United States have been very creative in terms of establishing non-profit and for-profit organizations more than any other South Sudanese divisions. Their intention was to take advantage of the opportunity available in United States to do something tangible collectively for their country, and the people left behind in the South Sudan. A noble idea. The Nuer people's creativity as new

Americans started with grouping themselves into churches in large numbers. This compelled American churches to assist them with buildings to enjoy sermons in their dialect. Ironically, these churches became the epicenter of the community's destruction.

The leaders of this community were being guided by self-interest and indigenous cultural mind sets while being ignorant of leadership principles. I and my uncle, the late John Kang, witnessed this behavior at the Sudanese Evangelical Covenant Church's reconciliation conference in Omaha, Nebraska in 2004. Church pastors and representatives traveled from many cities to Omaha for this conference, hoping that they could resolve their outstanding issues. All except the late Reverend John Phillip Pidak Lieth spoke along clannish lines supporting their clannish pastors in the Church of Jesus Christ.

Finally, my uncle John Kang and I were given a chance to speak. We were different from everybody else because our opinions targeted the issues being discussed, not people. As a result we were chosen to lead the next reconciliation meeting. I was nominated to the chair and my late uncle, John Kang was nominated to keep the minutes and maintain the records. During this meeting I realized that transparent leadership was lacking in this community. There was no unifying leader that clannish individuals would look up to for answers to issues facing the community daily.

The division of the church filtered down to the ethnic establishments, such as the community based organizations. This has begun with the Nasir Community Association in the United States (NCA-USA), which was established for infrastructure development in South Sudan. NCA-USA succeeded in raising more than two hundred thousand US dollars, from individual contributions only. Each member committed to contribute a certain amount each year at the annual conferences. The Maiwut community, Lou Nuer community, Fangak community, and Bentiu community have done the same, although they have not been as successful in comparison to the NCA-USA. The largest and best established, for-profit organization with hundreds of thousands of dollars ... the giant, NCA-USA was struck down into splinters like a giant tree ... its limbs broken into pieces as though it was in a free fall ... benefiting the firewood gatherers.

The NCA-USA's net income of thousands of dollars became a liability rather than an asset because of the lack of understanding of the leadership function. The split of this giant ethnic based organization has factored into many small sub-clannish establishments. Other ethnic organizations, such the Lou Nuer, Maiwut Nuer, Fangak Nuer, and Bentiu Nuer communities, followed the same patterns and destroyed their clannish establishments prematurely without achieving their intended goals.

Nuer have also established non-profits, 501 (c) 3 organizations, such as the South Sudanese Community Center of Omaha Nebraska. This organization used to have a budget of hundreds of thousands of dollars supported by government grants. The funding was to service the needs of the refugees and immigrants, not only the Sudanese, but other nationalities as well. Leadership principles have not been understood well by this community. Every person wanted to lead. Mistakenly leadership was interpreted in a coercive fashion. There was a perception of a kingdom, dominated by one family and the rest were expected to become servants and subordinate to the kings. They did not understand that it was the other way around. The leaders were supposed to be serving the communities. Instead of moving forward and into modern civilization, they were moving backward.

The lack of leadership and sub-divided clannish establishments have resulted in organized fundraiser parties. The intent of these fundraisers was infrastructure development of South Sudan. The fundraiser party attendance has been mandatory for all members to attend. These clannish parties take turns almost every month. There is one party after another. Children are left home alone. Parents are spending more than their means for donations bringing damage to the community as opposed to benefit. Families have not been able to save for their children's needs due to these non-stop fundraiser parties.

Due to mandatory attendance, children are often left unattended, without enough food, while their parents spend days and nights at parties. For the first time in South Sudanese tradition, night clubbing has become a hobby for both parents and children alike. When a man or a woman married, he/she retired from those things immediately because it is awkward for a married person to be seen in clubs. Day time activities, such as wedding and plays are okay for both parents and their children in the South Sudanese tradition. This has completely changed in the United States. For this reason parents are no longer demonstrating responsible behavior.

Enormous issues have surfaced in the marriages of the South Sudanese families in the United States due to the excessive parties. South Sudanese youth in the United States have used this opportunity of having no parents around all night long and taken advantage of it to go out with other boys or girls at night. Because of this Cultural Revolution, 70% of the Nuer families in the midwestern cities of the United States are not stable. This is especially true in Omaha, Nebraska. Significant increases in divorce rates, school dropouts, gang activities, and homelessness have been witnessed for the first time in Sudanese culture. These activities have disturbed me so much to the point that I wanted to do something that could help turn around this community, so the result is this book.

Domestic Violence Law and South Sudanese Families

Marital dispute or fight within the marriage is often undermined in Sudanese community to be a serious matter as Americans call it "Domestic Violence." The Sudanese undermined this because it is considered the cultural way of disciplining the wife, not only in the Sudanese community, but also in many cultures. Marital dispute is not considered a crime, and often refugees and immigrants' women do not know that they can report a physical fight as an abuse.

Because the Sudanese's cultural way of life has not been understood by the US government as part of their normal life in United States, domestic violence victim agencies that handle cases from refugee populations provide victims with counseling on coping with the effects of domestic violence and encourage the victims to report anything including verbal fighting to police. The services being offered to the victims of crime includes counseling, designing safety plans for the women by identifying whom to call for help, making copies of their important documents, and making extra sets of keys in case of emergencies. In addition, the agencies advise the women to seek for a solution to end this ongoing violence; therefore, the easy solution to the Sudanese women is to let go the perpetrators.

Another aspect of this service is providing shelter referrals for women who are in need of crisis intervention. This assistance actually encourages the split of families.

Sudanese women who decide that they want to leave domestic abuse situations design long-term self-sufficiency plans with the aid of the agencies, such as developing job search skills in order to attain financial independence, but they are not always successful in becoming independent. Domestic violence victims are also instructed on the legal process, particularly focusing on such areas as child support, child custody, and getting a restraining order against their men.

This brings to an end the South Sudanese family happiness and turns upside down the whole family instead. In the most cases, the law enforcement agencies face issues in providing the counseling services that they promised to the families affected by domestic violence. Locating or equipping personnel with the appropriate multicultural skills may prove challenging. Finding caseworkers to deal with domestic violence issues in the South Sudanese population is difficult due to the fact that many are not employed by the local social services to provide services to their own people. The lack of employing personnel in this community is not associated with an insufficiency of needed skills, but hiring a community liaison was regarded as unimportant. In this challenging environment in the South Sudanese families diaspora, mental illness is silently affecting the majority of people.

Change of "attitude" was preached to the Nuer community by Mr. Thowath Pal Chay; therefore, sharing duties in the house is important and part of changing attitude. Verbal fighting is even a better alternative to physical fighting. Fighting in the marriage is normal because each has to be assertive and claim his/her right.

Why is sharing important to the family? Getting off work from a meat factory or from another industry, going straight home to start cooking, cleaning, giving children a bath and so forth can be overwhelming for one person. Sharing in this matter would mean that whoever happens to be home at this point should help out with household chores instead of waiting for only one person to do these. Positive communication would mean being true to one another by sharing finances. Couples should communicate their concerns with open hearts as often as needed. They should put all their finances on the table and decide together who will be given some money in Africa, perhaps to both a husband and a wife's families and friends equally. Both husband and wife should respect and care for one another and appreciate one another rather than putting one or the other down verbally or physically. It is even an awesome thing to learn to apologize when you are at fault for the sake of peace and to put the issue to rest.

In seeking help from a professional or from a person of your choice before a situation get out of control is a safety net for both husband and wife. One of the issues may be suspicion of an affair in marriage, wrongdoing with the family finances or lack of effective children discipline, which may involve parents to take sides with children. A professional third party would be a family counselor in your area, a church pastor in your community, or your parents if they happen to be around. This outside help could be eye opening and reveal a better way of managing your situation. If you utilize these steps, you will minimize your issues or eliminate them for good.

Nuer's Pioneers Speak Out

Thowath Pal Chay

I have had an opportunity to meet uncle Thowath Pal Chay for the second time in San Diego during his visit to the United States of America in 2007. Mr. Thowath Pal Chay met with the South Sudanese Nuer Community on July 25, 2007. He helped address some issues facing them; he wanted them to understand and change their behaviors. The primary purpose of his meeting was to educate the Nuer people to change their attitudes. I served as his secretary, taking the minutes of the meeting. Enclosed in this book is his meeting's minutes trying to help the Nuer people understand this modern way of life. The purpose of attaching the minutes is to validate what I have talked about throughout this book, changing the way of life or attitude. This is the evidence that it is very challenging in this community to persuade members to adapt healthy attitudes.

Mr. Thowath Pal was welcomed on stage and given an opportunity to brief the gathering. He introduced a series of messages including what Nuer have in common and what they can do together while overcoming the challenges of managing two different political ideologies. His objective of helping turn around the South Sudanese community had a special focus on Nuer people's attitude. Thowath Chay introduced a proposal to create an organization to serve as a symbol of the change.

He preached, "I am giving you a proposal for a (Nuer International Cultural Orientation Center) as something that will unite all Nuer wherever they live, around the globe. What I want to share with you is that, we need to accept that we have problems that we have to find ways to resolve them. We're in between two organizations or governments, and we have limited our participation wherever we live." Mr. Thowath was implying the Ethiopian and South Sudanese governments, but also the United States government. "We need to open our limitation so that we know who we are. All problems started from Nuer Land, am I right?"

Mr. Thowath Pal has elaborated more on the constitution, that it can assist Nuer to open their eyes and overcome their issues. He also pointed out that Nuer people have a lot of achievements, but remain as part of the underclass. Nuer are 96-thousands within the population of 80-million Ethiopian, so the meaning of "international" is that you live or belong to more than two countries. "My message to you is that you're belonging to the United States of America, so if you don't work here, you will not work in Sudan as well. Therefore, we need to change our attitude. What we have talked about in 2005 has formulated to something practical, the constitution. This organization is non-political, so it is up to us to keep what we have discussed today whether we go ahead with it or leave it."

Second, Mr. Thowath presented "10 Ways to Wreck Work," which he believes is the absolute reason why people fail to be committed to anything. Mr. Thowath introduced the second handout and titled "Seven Deadly Sins." Mr. Thowath elaborated that Nuer are capable of accomplishing anything. They simply thwart themselves. He also said that people who have been fighting for political parties in South Sudan are Nuer; therefore we need to know the definition of leadership that is a collective of ideas. Mr. Thowath Pal stopped his briefing at this point and allowed people to ask questions. I identified social problems, and facilitated questions.

Pastor Peter Lual cited several problems in the community. Disobedient children and women were blamed. Clergy trainees calling themselves pastors before they were ordained and working in the community were also singled out as a problem. "I want you to help us orient women and their children and advise those who have bought a symbol of pastoral ordination, "collar or Dok" in Nuer to stop calling themselves pastors until they are ordained." Pastor Peter reiterated that this behavior has never ever happened in Nuer culture before.

These people are shameless now because they have lost their cultural values. They are confusing others with regard to the pastoral title. What is real and what is not real in the pastoral community is now unfocused. Peter Biel Lual pointed out that hatred and resentment will never take us anywhere. We must help other people in our community. "If you're not agreeing with your wife, you're a dead man."

Uncle Peter Biel encouraged people to embrace peace and good governance from their homes or community before they reach out to help others outside of their homes and community. Nyayul Kuon asked "Murle is chasing people and destroying our home villages, so where are you going to find people?" Nyayul Kuon asked Thowath Pal if the politicians should protect the civilians. Thomas Nyang, stated "Our children are our future, but now they're not obeying because they are not going to school or listening to their parents, so what can we do as parents." Sarah Nyakuach Gach stated "We need to enforce love among ourselves, so let us change our way of communication with our husbands", referring to women. Sarah Nyakuach elaborated on the point of that Peter Biel and Thomas Nyang rose about the family issue, "Change must start from the husband and wife for their children to mimic the same behavior."

Peter Koang Gatkuoth asked a question regarding the formation of a new Nuer community and indicated that "There is a Nuer community already in existence!" He stated, "This is another Nuer community, so we need to change one name and consolidate our names." Peter Koang pointed out the fact that neither one of these communities will work because there is hatred and jealousy among the Nuer people. General assembly is the problem, so this attitude has to change; people whom have been elected leaders are not being respected by their followers. As a former leader of the Nasir Community Association of the United States, Peter Koang has expressed exactly what is going on in the community.

Leaders have a hard time enforcing the rules. Peter reiterated "People will agree on something verbally and never act on it." Nyachan Kang has only read the Bible to encourage people to listen to what God wants them to do, love and forgive one another. She was expressing her frustration on what she has been seeing in the community. Peter Lam Thot reiterated the point highlighted earlier by Peter Koang Gatkuoth. Mr. Lam asked, "As we have Nuer Communities in all states, did you consult Nuer leaders about the formation of this organization?" The question was directed to Mr. Thowath Pal.

Lam Thot added "Nuer International Cultural Orientation Center is good, but dialogue is needed to identify the right direction." Thowath Pal answered "People who want to lead always have a system, so Nuer needs that for them to survive among other

Sudanese. Nuer have a lot of interests that are not helping them, so (Army General) Paulino Matip Nhial is one of the alternatives for Nuer's survival in the South Sudan Government. In terms of consultation with other Nuer leaders in the United States, yes I want them to be the beneficiary of this organization. This will help them lead the right way." Ester Peter Biel Lual advised children to listen to their parents. Dep Nhial Tuany: stated "I am going to talk about this new organization that our brother Mr. Thowath Pal Chay has come with. Before, Evangelist Bapal Gak Deng came with Nuer Christian Network; we did accept it."

Dep has also reminded people that today, if Mr. Thowath Pal comes with this organization, we have to accept it as well. Dep was reminding people that they should be fair to all of those who want to exercise their desire to help the Nuer people in one way or another. He also asked a question to Mr. Thowath Pal to help advise young generations "To me, let us support this idea even if we're not going to support it financially." Again, Dep Tuany raised another issue about the churches' problem, referring to the Sudanese Community Religious Service of San Diego, a union of all Sudanese churches in San Diego and referred the matter to Mr. Thowath Pal to look at and advise the church leaders as well.

Thuok Chuol Bol expressed his overwhelming appreciation to Thowath's willingness to help the community and suggested that if the community could duplicate our brother Mr. Thowath Pal, a lot of our problems would come to an end in a short time.

Unfortunately, Thuok said that we cannot do it. All we need to do is to take what he is telling us and use it for our own benefit. Nyaleak Diew provided advice and reflected upon a division that exists among the people. Moses Lam Mark pointed out that (NICOE) is different from the organizations that we already have, so he accepted the idea to support this organization. Peter Gatkuoth Gak expressed his opinion that if he were to influence the people's ideas, he would accept this new organization. Mr. Gak went further and criticized women about using their children against their fathers.

He reflected the problem to Mr. Thowath to address it. John Chuol Kuek stated " I don't think that having another Nuer organization would be a great idea. What we need to do is provide technical support to the organizations that we already have to make them better. Nuer community needs all the programs that Mr. Thowath Pal has created in this constitution." John Kuek elaborated further, "I am speaking based on my experience in this community that if we create a new organization, both new and old Nuer communities will simply just die. I am afraid to commit to something that will not function; I am not against this organization, but I am telling you something that you will realize later if you agree to form this organization on top of the existing Nuer community."

Both Chol stated "I do support what John Kuek has said already about incorporating Mr. Thowath's programs into the Nuer community, but not creating another one." Nyapal Gatdoar: "We need Nuer culture to teach our children, so this idea is good." Mabil Jock: "We have a problem; our problem is that when we agree to something, we do not follow up. We need to brief Mr. Thowath Pal about many organizations that already exist. If we are saying that we want to create another one, this is a joke because it is not going to work." Kuachuor Mark: "We do not need to talk about our problems here, so if you need help about your own problem, call pastor to your home so that he will pray for you."

Kuachuor was referring to Peter Gak's statement criticizing women for mobilizing their children against their fathers. Mr. Thowath Pal Chay was given an opportunity to answer these questions, so Mr. Thowath started by reflecting that people resistance change and they do not like to change their attitudes. Mr. Thowath made it clear to people that he is going to work with Nuer Community and Nuer Christian Mission Network. His advised the members that they need to stop calling themselves Lou, Gaajiok or Gaajaak (sub cultural divisions of Neur) because it's a limitation. The meeting was attended by 57 people in San Diego.

By reading these minutes, one can see the struggle this community has been facing. It is in need of rescue. Many things need to change in this community. Change will not be realized unless members focus on documents like this one to see for themselves the peril that the community faces. Even protocols as simple as time keeping meet resistance. A person attempting to

45

enforce rules is regarded as tyrannical. This community is victimized by anarchists and needs guidance to focus on love, cooperation and the principals of nonviolent communication.

Prepared by John Chuol Kuek
Copyright: Nuer International Cultural Orientation Center (NICOE)
Created in San Diego, CA/7/25/07 for the first time in United States of America

The Vice President, Dr. Riek Machar

I was able to have a phone conversation with the Vice President of the Republic of South Sudan, Dr. Riek Machar, regarding the opportunities for the diasporas in the new nation. Dr. Machar started by asking me, "What are you doing, John?" I answered his question with another question, "Do you mean what I am doing for a living or my education?" he answered, "both." I finally answered him that I am working as counselor or (marriage and family counselor). He answered, "That is very good John, and this is what I told people in Omaha, Nebraska during my meeting with them. The country needs counselors to help people including the government officials such as the leadership, because our people need to reconcile with one another."

In his meeting in Omaha Nebraska, Dr. Riek Machar spoke of trauma in South Sudan, saying that even among the senior leadership there are some who are suffering from post-traumatic stress disorder. He suggested all senior officials in the Government of South Sudan should seek counseling. He stressed that all of them have been in war for a long time, and many of them are demonstrating dysfunctional behavior and they need rehabilitation to reintegrate into normal life.

The Republic of South Sudan is committed to building institutions that will seek to address post-war traumatic stress disorder, he said. Dr. Machar's statement reiterates the fact of what needs to happen, not only in our country, but also in Sudanese communities worldwide. The reason I resonate with Dr. Machar's statement is because I believe in the change of attitude as preached by uncle Thowath Pal Chay in Nuer community meetings all over the United States. Profit is not my motivation. Improvement of my people's condition is my motivation. I am happy that my people are finally realizing the hidden truth. To realize peace in our country, we must reconcile with one another.

Suggestions for Families and Counselors

Parents possess greater wisdom than their children. Parents must approach children in effective ways. They must avoid putting them down because of a bad grade or a mistake. They must always treat them with respect. Children are wonderful. They respond well to friendly behavior whether it's from inside the family or outside. Parents desiring their children to be familiar with South Sudanese culture must sit down with them and tell stories about values and traditions. It is integral that parents reflect strongly on the intrinsic value of respecting their elders, especially elderly people.

Children should be shown that parents understand their rights and feelings when discussing issues. Parents should not avoid discussing critical issues, including sexual behavior and dating boys and girls. Wise parents will not pretend as if these behaviors do not exist. This reflects ignorance of facts about life. Effective parents will demonstrate knowledge of factors that may make their children feel uncomfortable when reflecting on South Sudanese culture. Children who are respected and supported are more likely to understand and respects parental rights, values and traditions.

Effective parents are a child's best teacher, role model and protector in his/her life. Parents should demonstrate love and care toward their children. Children treated in this fashion are less likely to seek and find comfort outside of their homes.

Children need education and support to avoid incest. Parents should know their children's friends and protect them from online predators by monitoring their computer use. Concerned parents will help their children with their homework. Additional support can be obtained from homework clubs in the neighborhood. Parents can research them and assign children there to get help. Compassionate and loving parents demonstrate patience for their childrens' efforts regardless of the grade. A "D or F" grade they received from class could be met with a comment like "You will do better next time", or "How can I support you more". They will do better with your support.

Compassionate and effective parents avoid forcing their ideas on their children to choose a career of the parent's choice. This choice should be based on the child's interests since they will be making a career choice that will affect the rest of their lives. Many refugee and immigrant parents who prefer their children to be doctors, engineers, or lawyers because of the past traumatic experience they came from: support them in their career of choice regardless. It is recommended that counseling services be sought out as a source of support. One of the questions that might be asked is "What is counseling?" Where some parents grew up, counseling may not be one of the services families have experienced.

Counseling is not new in South Sudanese culture. It simply was not called "counseling". Strong family support systems provided this need in traditional South Sudanese families. This is more difficult today with the diasporas that have been created. Elder advice remain a very important component in South Sudanese families. In the Western world all of the above are true and have been incorporated into professional advice or counseling. The next chapter will familiarize you with terms that are intrinsic to understanding counseling and how it might benefit families.

CHAPTER 4

Counseling

ॐ

Individual Therapy

Individual therapy refers to therapy sessions with one client and one therapist. Individual sessions with a therapist average about 45 minutes to one hour long. An alternative to group therapy, individual therapy is offered in many different types or branches of psychology. Psychology is the science of understanding human behavior, thought, emotion and perception. Therapy strives to help people better understand themselves and their problems in order to cope with the demands of their daily lives.

In the counseling field, there are many models. Cognitive Behavioral Therapy is one example. This therapeutic model examines thoughts, feelings and behaviors, and the relationships and patterns between them. In individual cognitive behavioral therapy, the therapist works with the client to set goals for coping with problems in the client's life. This may involve replacing negative thought patterns with positive ones or the goal may be steps to take to face a specific fear, such as flying in an airplane. Psychodynamic or psychoanalytic therapies strive for personal growth through insight into the subconscious as well as the conscious mind.

The therapist uses techniques such as word association to help reveal feelings and wishes that may add insight into the client's actions and conscious thoughts. Since the focus in this type of therapy is on the mind and inner workings of the individual, psychoanalytic therapies are traditionally and typically done on an individual rather than group therapy basis.

Group Therapy

Whereas in group therapy the clients listen to others' problems and breakthroughs, people in individual therapy are focused only on their own situation. Both types of therapy may be helpful to patients, depending on their problem as well as their therapeutic preference. Personal growth can be an outcome of both individual and group therapy. In some group therapy cases, hearing about the experiences of others who have a similar problem can provide helpful insight that allows a therapy client to think about his or her own experiences in a different way. Yet, individual therapy may be more beneficial for a client who is likely to be distracted from focusing on changing his or her own behavior to create a healthier and more peaceful situation in his or her life. The decision to choose either individual therapy or group therapy is an important one that should be made carefully.

Family Therapy

Family therapy involves a whole family, or several family members, all meeting with a therapist. Family therapy can be helpful if a family is having problems getting along. It can also be used with one family member who has a problem. Family relationships may be contributing to or maintaining the problem. In many cases the problem may be exhibited by a child, but this is not always the case. Family therapy is often recommended if a child has a behavior problem. Some family therapists see the child with the problem as the "scapegoat" and view the problem as actually residing within the family system. Eating disorders in adolescents are often treated with family therapy. Family therapists avoid blaming any family member for the problems; rather, they help the family interact in different ways that may solve the problem.

Family therapy is based on the belief that the family is a unique social system with its own structure and patterns of communication. These patterns are determined by many factors, including the parents' beliefs and values, the personalities of all family members, and the influence of the extended family (grandparents, aunts, and uncles). As a result of these variables, each family develops its own unique personality, which is powerful and affects all of its members.

Family therapy is based on the concepts that illness in one family member may be a symptom of a larger family problem. To treat only the member who is identified as ill is like treating the symptom of a disease but not the disease itself. It is possible that if the person with the illness is treated but the family is not, another member of the family will become ill. This cycle will continue until the problems are examined and treated. Any change in one member of the family affects both the family structure and each member individually. Health professionals who use the family systems model in caring for people always consider the whole family. They view any problem in one member as a symptom of change or conflict in the group.

A family therapist:

• Teaches family members about how families function in general and, in particular, how their own family functions.

• Helps the family focus less on the member who has been identified as ill and focus more on the family as a whole.

• Assists in identifying conflicts and anxieties and helps the family develop strategies to resolve them.

• Strengthens all family members so they can work on their problems together.

• Teaches ways to handle conflicts and changes within the family differently.

Sometimes the way family members handle problems makes them more likely to develop symptoms. During therapy sessions, the family's strengths are used to help them handle their problems. All members take responsibility for problems. Some family members may need to change their behavior more than others.

Family therapy is a very active type of therapy, and family members are often given assignments. For example, parents may be asked to delegate more responsibilities to their children. The number of sessions required varies, depending on the severity of the problems and the willingness of the members to participate in therapy. The family and the therapist set mutual goals and discuss the length of time expected to achieve the goals. Not all members of the family attend each session.

Child Therapy

Child therapy is a form of therapy that has been tailored for children. Children can sometimes benefit from psychotherapy. Versions of physiotherapy, speech therapy, and other types of therapy are also available for children. Parents may seek therapy for their children on the recommendation of a doctor. For example, a doctor could suggest physical therapy for a child who has been burned so that the child can recover his or her range of motion. In this case the parents can also seek out therapy on their own to deal with issues which arise as the child develops.

In the case of psychotherapy, child therapy can be offered by a psychologist, psychiatrist, counselor, or licensed clinical social worker. Group and solo therapy are available for children, along with directed therapy with parent and child to discuss specific behavioral issues. Every therapist has a unique approach to working with children, and may integrate several therapeutic techniques to find one which works for the child, including play therapy, cognitive behavioral therapy, or music therapy.

Children in a wide variety of situations can benefit from psychotherapy. Behavioral issues can sometimes be a sign of underlying psychological problems, and children who are struggling in school may also be candidates for therapy. Stressful events such as the death of a parent, a big move, or a parental deployment can all be occasions for a few sessions of therapy to help the child process the event.

The various types of physical therapy used in rehabilitation of adults are also available to children in child therapy. Children who have experienced traumatic brain injuries, broken limbs, burns, and other traumatic physical events may attend sessions with a physical therapist to help regain their prior strength. Congenital birth defects which lead to issues like speech impediments or cognitive impairments can also be addressed with therapy. Some practitioners specialize in child therapy, working in settings like children's hospitals, while others treat children and adults.

Finding a good therapist for a child can be a challenge. Just like adults, children sometimes need to try several therapists to find a good fit. Therapy, whether it's for a broken leg or a broken heart, will not progress unless the child feels comfortable with the therapist. Parents may want to interview the therapist first to get a feel for how the therapist works and how the therapist approaches child therapy sessions, and then ask for a trial appointment so that the child can meet with the therapist without the pressure of being committed to future appointments.

Teen Issues and Solutions

South Sudanese are part of the Western World's culture; therefore, we cannot ignore issues facing our children and ourselves in daily basis. It had never been an issue in the South Sudan that children drink alcohol and do drugs, but now they do. Nobody can deny that teen's behavior is the same every country. Teenager behavior is similar no matter which culture one happens to grow up in. In any culture, there is nothing more frustrating to parents than to know something serious is going on with their teen, but to have absolutely no idea what the problem is.

I encourage every parent to contact a therapist and discuss parenting strategies for getting to the bottom of your teen's issues, as well as provide information about counseling and adolescent treatment programs. Parents should be the first to detect changes and problems in their teenager. If parents are preoccupied with conflict among themselves, they may not be effective in this area. If it doubtful that they will be able to follow their kids and monitor their behaviors. Knowing the differences between normal teenage behavior and understanding when it is time to seek help for a troubled teen can be a very delicate task.

The problem lies in the fact that the teen years are filled with changes, and sometimes teenagers who are acting normally can appear to be troubled, especially to parents who have enjoyed a good relationship with their child until he/she became a teenager. Knowing when intervention of a professional counselor is necessary is an important part of being the parents of a teenager. It requires careful vigilance and the ability to recognize when a teen's behavior is appearing to get out of hand, or when his/her life appears to be incongruent.

Most teenagers go through changes at this point. Some may not want to interact more often with their parents. There are some signs to look for that could indicate that your teen's behavior goes beyond normal teenager's quest for independence and experimentation including:

• Changing friends abruptly, or becoming a loner.

• Anxiety and depression, beyond normal ups and downs.

• Dramatic change in performance at school.

• Desire to constantly miss school.

Destructive Behavior

• Hurting self or others.

• Cruelty to animals.

• Vandalism.

• Preoccupation with death.

• Signs of teenage alcohol or drug abuse.

Other Signs

• Obsession with weight or being fat, even when weight is considered normal.

• Constant complaints about physical images.

• Difficulty in coping with daily life.

• Dramatic changes in sleeping habits or eating patterns.

• Mood swings.

• Increasingly argumentative, defensive and violent.

It is important to note that normal teenager behavior does include some feelings of being an outsider, and arguments with family members. The key is to look for an increasing occurrence of the troubled teen's behavior, and to look for signs that some of the behavior could be related to teen alcohol or drug abuse, or to the emergence of a mental or psychological disorder. It can be difficult to distinguish between normal teen behavior and troubled teen behavior. This is because so often teenagers begin changing into their own people, and because some of what they do and listen to seems alien to parents.

One thing you can do is to observe current teenage trends at the school your teenager attends. For instance, lowering pants and ear piercings may not indicate troubled behavior. These could be popular styles. When you drop your teenager off at school or attend parent-teacher conferences, make sure you observe the styles. If your teen's style is mostly in line with the popular peer-group, chances are that he or she is exhibiting normal teenage behavior.

If, however, you notice a dramatic drop in quality of schoolwork accompanying the physical changes, it could be a sign of a troubled teen. If your teen is involved with alcohol and drug abuse, or if he/she appears to be suffering from anxiety or depression, it is important to get help from a professional. Talk to your teen about how you are concerned for him or her. Tell them you would like to find out if there is a way that he or she can be helped by a third person. Seek a professional evaluation.

Drug and Alcohol Use Warning Signs

Experimentation with drugs and alcohol is common now in the West even in Africa. The abuse of drugs and alcohol by teenagers continues to increase. This section reviews how to detect drug and alcohol use's warning signs and some of the risk factors for youth alcohol and drug abuse.

How can you detect that your teen is using alcohol or illicit drugs? According to Diller and Diller (2003), there are various warning signs of teenage drug and alcohol abuse. Watching for these signs can help you identify a problem with a teenager that you may know. It is important, however, to recognize that some of the signs associated with teen alcohol and drug use are also associated with other conditions, such as depression and childhood disorders that many South Sudanese parents are not aware of.

Your child might exhibit one of these disorders: Attention Deficit Disorder (ADD), Attention Deficit Hyperactivity Disorder (ADHD), Oppositional Defiant Disorder (ODD), and Conduct Disorder (CD). There are more childhood disorders not included in this book, but this is just to give you an idea of what some of our children are going through like any other children in the Western World.

Diagnostic and Statistical Manual of Mental Disorders, Fourth Edition, Text Revision (DSM-IV-TR, 2000) provides a brief descriptions of these disorders: Attention deficit hyperactivity disorder (ADHD or ADD) is a developmental disorder. It is primarily characterized by "the co-existence of intentional problems and hyperactivity, with each behavior occurring infrequently alone" and symptoms starting before seven years of age. ADHD is the most commonly studied and diagnosed psychiatric disorder in children, affecting about 3-5% of children globally and diagnosed in about 2-16% of school aged children. It is a chronic disorder with 30-50% of those individuals diagnosed in childhood continuing to have symptoms into adulthood (Diller & Diller, 2003).

Oppositional Defiant Disorder (ODD) is a childhood disorder that is characterized by negative, defiant, disobedient and often hostile behavior toward adults and authority figures primarily. In order to be diagnosed, the behaviors must occur for at least a period of 6 months. Oppositional Defiant Disorder is characterized by the frequent occurrence of at least four of the following behaviors:

• Losing temper.

• Arguing with adults.

• Actively defying or refusing to comply with the requests or rules of adults.

• Deliberately doing things that will annoy other people.

• Blaming others for his or her own mistakes or misbehavior.

• Being touchy or easily annoyed by others.

• Being angry and resentful.

• Being spiteful or vindictive.

The usual pattern is for problems to begin between ages 1-3. Conduct Disorder (CD) is a group of behavioral problems where a child is aggressive, antisocial and defiant to a much greater degree than expected for your child's age. Characteristics of conduct disorder include:

• Fighting and physical cruelty.

• Destructiveness, such as setting fire at home school.

• Lying and stealing.

• Truancy (including running away from home).

To get a diagnosis of conduct disorder, your child must have shown at least three of these characteristics over the past year, with at least one of the characteristics shown in the last six months. This disorder begins before age 13. A proper diagnosis by a doctor can be helpful.

Emotional signs of teen alcohol and drug abuse: sudden mood swings, irresponsible behavior, lack of interest in activities of former interest, personality differences, low self-esteem, and irritability.

Physical signs of teen alcohol and drug abuse: repeated health problems, lingering cough, fatigue, frequent headaches, red and gazed eyes.

Social indications of teenage drug and alcohol abuse: changes in friends and preferred activities, changes in style of dress, less attention to personal appearance, run-ins with the law, and taking money or valuables from the home.

School problems associated with teenage alcohol and drug abuse: dropping grades, discipline problems, frequent trips to the principal, decreased interest in school activities and extracurricular activities, truancy, increased tardiness, and negative attitude.

Family problems associated with teen drug and alcohol abuse: withdrawing deliberately from the family, violent outbursts, starting arguments, breaking curfew or sneaking out at night, and breaking family rules.

Treatment of teen alcohol and drug abuse usually includes in or out patient treatment for withdrawal symptoms and counseling for psychological dependency. Support of friends and family is vital while a teenager is recovering from alcohol and drug abuse.

Suicide Warning Signs

In Sudanese tradition, one may say "I will kill you or kill myself," this is not taken seriously because it has been part of the culture to say so, but now we live in the Western world where deadly issues associated with this threat have been witnessed by all the refugees and immigrants.

We cannot deny that our culture has changed, and we have two different generations in our families. Therefore, it is worth educating the community about explicit suicide warning signs so we can be aware. Explicit suicide warning signs include the situation in which a person threatens to kill others or self. In addition to being a real threat, this may also be a very disturbing exhibition of manipulation, for example, if someone were to say, "If you leave me, I will kill myself." However, if you hear something like this, do not ignore it. Stop and consider what the motivation is and call for help immediately.

I want you to keep this in mind though, a person could also mention hurting or killing him or herself without a means or an identified method, no matter the possible causes, help should be sought immediately (Diller & Diller, 2003).

These are tips with the intention of educating the community so that they take advantage of the therapeutic services available in their areas. Most the family issues, such as those described in this book, can be handled by counseling. Counseling is part of healthy activities that any person needs to balance family and professional life. Counseling is not for mentally unstable individuals only; therefore, I hope you and your family change your attitude by taking this advice so seriously for your own benefits.

CHAPTER 5

Culturally Sensitive Practices

ℬ

Culturally sensitive practice begins with an assessment of the culture that the client identifies with. In describing Sudanese culturally sensitive practices, Sudan is a miniature representation of Africa: a large country, before it was divided into two geographic extremes ranging from sandy desert to tropical forest. It has about 600 tribes who have Arabic as their common language. There are about 142 different languages (Duany, 2000).

The cuisine is a melding of many varied backgrounds of the people who live in the Sudan's land. With this brief background of the Sudan introduced, there is also the notion that people are the same in some ways despite their cultures. While humans share some characteristics in terms of biology and emotion, research has shown that other experiences may be different, such as how depression, anxiety, grief, loss, and the communication of emotions in the family are manifested differently in different cultures (Kapolo, 2001). With this chapter, Sudanese's culturally sensitive practices are discussed.

Current Literature

In Sudan, human life centers on the family and the extended family system. This belief forms the basis for social relations and behaviors in the entire kinship system. Without a clear knowledge and understanding of the social structure of the family system, supporting organizations and therapists will fail to provide proper counseling and psychotherapy to the family in crisis whether in Africa, North America, or the other parts of the world. Within the entire Sudanese culture, the family system is changing because of urbanization and industrialization (Kapolo, 2001). Nevertheless, old habits die hard in Sudanese culture. Thus, Sudanese family crises cannot be dealt with adequately within the framework of Western family systems, especially those of Europe and North America.

While the Sudanese have a set of core values, it does not mean Sudan has nothing to learn from the way the Western family operates, just as the West can no doubt learn from Sudan. According to Kapolo (2001), the church in its ministry of healing and counseling is in a good position to create a family counseling model based on an understanding of the Sudanese culture. The only counseling service available to this population is through churches. Therefore, it is a duty of those Sudanese educated in the Western World to take what they learn back to South Sudan. Such a model would integrate the Sudanese concept of family care with Western-oriented family care.

Effective Interventions

Sudanese traditional family counselors believe that prevention is better than cure. Traditional Sudanese counseling begins with proper instruction before the marriage takes place. Such instruction will remain as a lifelong guidance for the new family. Although instruction varies in different communities, arranged marriages are common. The traditional Sudanese family counsel provides what they call marriage boundaries, instructed by the families of the bride and groom. The family, as an institution within the community, gives instructions on marriage and family life.

These marriage boundaries are a reminder to the new couple that they are about to enter an institution recognized in the community and approved by their relatives. Dishonoring such an institution brings shame to the family and community (Kapolo, 2001). The marriage boundaries urge the couple to have and act appropriately within the marriage framework. After the marriage boundary or institutional boundary for formation is finished, the family counsel discusses the relational boundaries.

These relational boundaries and interventions build mutual caring within the new family and free the new couple from the boundaries of the family of origin. Members of the family of origin are warned not to interfere in the family relationship of the new couple. Sudanese are community-oriented people. Particular situations have to be judged on the basis of their impact on the community. To avoid misunderstandings within the community, each family has the responsibility to instruct its members about the common goal of the entire community.

Phrases like "It takes a village to raise a child" and "I am, because you are" reflect the Sudanese way of life. The phrases also reflect the responsibility of the community to raise children together. A community as a social unit has common norms and boundaries that regulate communications, customs, and rituals. However, families also have norms and boundaries that regulate their own rules and behaviors. Parents, uncles, aunts, and grandparents form a group of responsible relatives, a family council, which instructs young people in family affairs. These responsible relatives function as keepers of family boundaries, counselors, and peacemakers. These family boundaries ground the family as a social unit (Duany, 2000).

According to the Sudanese family system, parents and all adults in the family have a responsibility to instruct youth in the kinds of work required for all purposes in life. Family formation begins with the process of finding a marriage partner, a process that includes parents and community members as well as the couple. The process begins like this: Sudanese believe that the family of origin has great influence on people, so in planning marriage they scrutinize the habits of the family of origin. A good relationship is needed not only between the two young people intending to marry but also between their families as well.

There are many models of therapy, however, many of them would not work for this population. There are some good therapeutic models which I recommend for any therapist working with members of this particular group. Those few therapies are cognitive behavioral, communication and other models with similar approaches. In this chapter the communication approach is used as an example of what works best in this culture.

The goal of communications family therapy, through engendering healthy family and individual communication, is to keep the family system in a healthy state of homeostasis, a healthy balance between change and stability. According to Satir (1988), maturity is one of the goals in therapy. The mature persons are able to accurately to perceive the world, make choices, accept personal responsibility for those choices, and communicate clearly. Such a person is unique, and recognizes them as different from others, but reacts to differences with eagerness as a learning opportunity, rather than a threat.

Mature people are aware of inner thoughts, feelings, and can let each other know what is going on. A dysfunctional person tends to communicate incongruently. Such people see the present through labels fixed from the early part of their lives. They strengthen these labels with each subsequent use. The present will be forced into the model of the past, or expectations of the future, rather than dealt with as it is. Dysfunctional people tend to have low self-esteem and unclear communication becomes a defense against dealing with and facing their low self-esteem (Satir, 1988).

Communication therapy defines the problem in clear and concrete terms: investigate all solutions for the problem that previously have been attempted; define the change to be achieved in clear and concrete terms; and formulate and implement a strategy for change. Mainly through the use of dyads, counselors teach the family to communicate in healthier ways. According to Satir (1988), the communication between the two is negated by conflicting communication styles resulting in a communication impasse that can deeply disturb functioning of the family system. If the husband and wife can discover a way to speak each other's language or communicate in such a way that can be understood by each party, they will have a 95% chance to solve their problem.

Less Effective Interventions

Psychoanalysis is a form of psychotherapy used by qualified psychotherapists to treat patients who have a range of mild to moderate chronic life problems. Boscolol, Cecchin, Hoffman, & Penn, (1987) state that this approach is related to a specific body of theories about the relationships between conscious and unconscious mental processes, and should not be used as a synonym for psychotherapy in general. Psychoanalysis is done one-on-one with the patient and the analyst; it is not appropriate for group work. In psychoanalytic treatment, the analyst is silent as much as possible, in order to encourage the patient's free association.

However, the analyst offers judiciously timed interpretations in the form of verbal comments about the material that emerges in the sessions (Boscolol et al, 1987). The therapist uses interpretations to uncover the patient's resistance to treatment, to discuss the patient's transference feelings, or to confront the patients with inconsistencies. Interpretations may be focused either on present issues, dynamic, or intended to draw connections between the patient's past and the present. Also, the patient is often encouraged to describe dreams and fantasies as sources of material for interpretation.

Psychoanalytic intervention will not help Sudanese clients because it focuses on early childhood, postulating that many of the conflicts arising in the human mind develop in the first years of a person's life. Freud demonstrated this in his theory of psychosexuality, in which the libido or sexual energy of the infant progressively seeks outlet through different body zones, such as oral, anal, phallic, and genital during the first five to six years of life (Boscolol et al, 1987). Sudanese culture is sensitive to anything related to sexuality and abuse. For these reasons, psychoanalysis and any similar theory or approach will likely not benefit Sudanese clients.

Effective Qualities of Therapists for This Population

Sue and Sue (1990), state that family counseling has been identified as one of the fastest-growing fields in psychology today. This treatment approach has been very effective because it encompasses many aspects of the family, which may include marriage counseling, parent-child counseling, or work with more than one member of the family. According to a review of the current literature on family therapy with Sudanese populations, one primary approach has been identified in family counseling, although there are a number of variations.

The approach is a communication therapy. Communication therapy is based on the assumption that family problems are communication difficulties. Many family communication problems are both subtle and complex (Sue & Sue, 1990). Family counselors in this theory concentrate on improving not only faulty communication, but also interactions and relationships among family members (Satir, 1988). The way in which rules, agreements, and perceptions are communicated among members is important (Haley, 2007). The counselor's role in repairing faulty communication is active, but not dominating.

According to Sue and Sue (1990), the culturally skilled counselors are those who have moved from being culturally unaware to being aware and sensitive to their own cultural heritage and to valuing and respecting differences. The counselors have begun the process of exploring their values, standards, and assumptions about human behavior. Rather than being ethnocentric and believing in the superiority of their group's cultural heritage such as arts, crafts, traditions, and language. Sue and Sue (1990) reiterate that the culturally skilled counselor should be aware of their own values and biases, and how they may affect minority clients. Counselors must have specific knowledge and information about the particular group they work with. In addition, counselors should have a good understanding of the sociopolitical system's operation in the United States with respect to its treatment of minorities (Sue & Sue, 1990).

Practical Steps to Resolving These Issues

South Sudanese people have developed destructive behaviors, which I don't think they understand. In the life time spectrum, it is impossible to answer every single question you hear on a daily basis. It is impossible to investigate every single item that comes to your attention. To grow, some issues need to be ignored. Failure to do this has resulted in lethal behaviors that affect our values unknowingly. We have damaged our families, churches, and other institutions. We have splintered and organized social and political organizations just because we have lost trust with each other. We need greater unity.

When it comes to interacting with our teens, avoid too much negativity and focus on what your teenager has done right. It is alright to correct your teen when he or she is wrong. Do so in a gentle manner, and accompany your critique with praise for some other activity that he or she is doing well. Make sure you recognize the good while you are helping to manage the bad. Focus on improvement, rather than on perfection. No one is going to be perfect. Let your teenager know that you notice when he or she makes improvements in their activities and behaviors. Focus on the journey, rather than what you wish was the end product. Encourage achievement and help your teenager set and achieve goals. They should be challenging goals, but also goals that your teen can accomplish.

Being able to overcome challenges and reach a goal can give your teenager a good sense of accomplishment and worth. Understand that your teenager may desire a different life and goals as opposed to what you want. You may want your teenager to be a doctor, but he or she may want to be a journalist or follow another profession. This is his or her choice. I want you to understand that your teen may have different goals in life. Try to support your teenager in his or her decisions. As long as your teen is not engaging in risky, damaging or illegal behavior, try to be supportive and encouraging.

Listen to your teen. Invite your teenager to share his or her ideas and opinions. Listen respectfully, and encourage critical thinking. Be a model of civil discussion and teach your teenager how to disagree without arguing.

Physical activity helps increase one's self esteem. Encourage your teenager to get regular exercise, either through activities at home or by participating in organized sports. Encourage extracurricular activities. Your teenager does not need to be involved in everything. One or two extra activities can really help improve self-esteem. It gives your teen something to improve and accomplish. Make sure you attend recitals, exhibitions and sporting events that your teenager participates in to show your support.

We need role models in the South Sudanese communities whose professions are congruent with their education and abilities. With great honor, I had the privilege to meet very fine young ladies from the Nuer community of Texas. Sarah Nyamuony Jock and Mary Nyangut Tap were introduced to the Nuer community of San Diego by Sarah Nyakuach Gach. My deepest gratitude goes to Sarah Nyakuach Gach for being of service to the community by connecting us with these fine young ladies.

I was amazed by the professionalism they demonstrated when speaking of concerns and issues facing the Nuer community. They spoke on very important issues, such as divorce, loss of cultural values, and how to retrieve wonderful Nuer traditional values that have been lost. They both encouraged ladies to avoid over reliance on 911 police rescue. They have used their personal lives as an example. They reiterated that your rescue is your own responsibility. Solving some issues in a traditional South Sudanese tradition will avoid destruction of the family unit as 911 police services could.

In addition to these ladies, I had the opportunity to work with three gentlemen who shined among the rest of the South Sudanese. Paulino Paida of the South Sudanese community of San Diego, and from Zande tribe of Equatoria regions in South Sudan. He coordinates the tuberculosis department for the health and human services in San Diego. Paulino earned a master's degree in Executive Business Administration from San Diego State University. He has been an outstanding individual in this community in terms of showing love, and leading by example. I had an opportunity to work with him on many different levels in the South Sudanese community of San Diego.

The second person is Joseph Jok of the South Sudanese community of San Diego, from Dinka tribe of the South Sudan. Joseph Jok is a graduate of the Alliant International University with a master's degree in an International Relations. Like Paulino Paida, I have had an opportunity to work with Joseph on many different levels in the South Sudanese community of San Diego as well, especially the 2010-2011 referendum of South Sudan. His leadership skills were excellent. Because of his leadership ability we achieved our intended goal of mobilizing, educating and succeeding toward voting with almost one hundred percent turnout during an election.

The third person was Gatluak Ter Thach of the Nashville Tennessee, from the Nuer tribe. Gatluak graduated with a master's degree in public service and a certificate of leadership and management. Gatluak is an executive director of the Nashville International Center for Empowerment. His organization is one of the leading non-profits, and is a community based organization dedicated to empowering refugees and immigrants who have resettled in Middle Tennessee through direct social services and educational programs. Like both Paulino and Joseph, I had an opportunity to know Gatluak since we were young, back in South Sudan. I met Gatluak again at the Office of the Refugees Resettlement Consultation Conference in Washington DC on September 1-2, 2011. Gatluak and I have discussed issues facing the community here in the United States.

We brainstormed topics germane to what can be done to turn this community around. Gatluak shared with me an example of a crisis we are facing in our families today. He said "I never ever in my life have seen married Nuer women going to parties or clubs from a distance unless they were joining a family marriage celebration. Traditionally they would go with their husbands and children. This is how it used to be, but this tradition has changed." Gatluak is one of the few South Sudanese working very hard to find ways to turn this community around. I admired him for his hard work and perseverence in maintaining this great organization despite obstacles from the community.

As one can see from the profiles of these three gentlemen, education is one of the best tools to help change this community around. I have had a blessed time with these highly educated South Sudanese men. Their leadership abilities reflect great credit upon their institution of education. It is important that more people become educated.

Here are some suggested, simple and practical steps intrinsic to help resolve issues facing the community:

1. We should all go to school, young and old, to learn and grow for sake of peace in our homes, community based organizations and the government.

2. Sharing duties in the house with your spouse will improve relationships for all members of the family.

3. Positive communication between married couples will help reduce tensions in the house.

4. Seek help from a professional or other appropriate person to help before a situation gets out of control.

5. Establish trust among community members across tribal and ethnic lines.

6. Provide opportunities to those who want to lead. Lend support and step up to the plate when it is your turn.

7. Set high goals for unity within the South Sudanese community as opposed to clinging on to tribal groups.

8. Prioritize your goals, focusing on your family first, then your community, and the country.

9. Spend more quality time with your spouse and your children to show them love.

10. Refrain from excessive attendance of parties. Save some money for your children.

11. Maintain your values and traditions for your children. Lead by example so your children will too.

12. Be resilient and learn to forgive. Show compassion to community members and be as positive as you can.

13. Try to minimize jealousy. Demonstrate praise and appreciation as widely as possible.

14. Change your "attitude" as uncle, Thowath Pal Chay had preached in the diaspora's Nuer Community.

15. Take advantage of being with your family to accomplish positive goals in your life.

16. When you view your family as an obstacle, it will be an obstacle. See your family as an opportunity, and you have a healthy family, and you will accomplish positive results.

CHAPTER 6

References

ဢ

American Psychological Association (2000). Diagnostic and Statistical Manual of Mental Health Disorders, Fourth Edition, Text Revision: Washington DC.

Baker, J. (2007). Forest Institute of Professional Psychology. Springfield: Missouri. U.S.A.

Bell, D. (1997). Defining of marriage and legitimacy. Current Anthropology, 38 (2) 237–254.

Boscolol, L., Cecchin, G., Hoffman, L., & Penn, p. (1987). Milan systemic family therapy: Conversation in Theory and Practice. New York: Basic Book Introduction from Psychoanalysis to systems.

Burton, J. W. (1995). Nuer Encyclopedia of World Cultures. Boston, Massachusetts: G K Hall and Co.

Baker, J. F. (2007). The divorce rate in America for first marriage, vs. second or third marriage. The Forest Institute of Professional Psychology.

Carisle, R. (1990). The Illustrated Encyclopedia of Mankind. NY: Marshall Cavendish.

Duany, J. A. (2000). The South Sudanese Lens. South Sudanese Friends International, 1, 2-6. (SSFI, Bloomington, Indian. U.S.A.

Diller. L. & Diller, L. H. (2003). Should I Medicated My Child? San solutions for troubled kids

Ember, C. R., & Melvin, E. (1998). Cultural Anthropology. Englewood Cliffs, New Jersey. Journal of Opinion, African Studies Association, 10, 4-12.

Enrichment Journal (2009). U.S.A.

Evans-Pritchard, E E. (1951). Kinship and Marriage among the Nuer. Oxford: Claredon Press.

Evan-Pritchard, E. E. (1948). Nuer Marriage Ceremonies Africa: Journal of the International African Institute 18, 29-40.

Ferraro, G. (2008). Cultural Anthropology: An Applied Perspective (7th Edition ed.). Belmont, CA, USA: Thomson Wadsworth.

Gashaw-Gant, G. G. (2004). Culture & Mental Health: a review of providing mental health services to East African Refugees and Immigrants. Alliant International University.

Gough, E. K. (1959). The nayars and the definition of marriage. Royal Anthropological Institute of Great Britain and Ireland, 89, 23-34.

Haley, J. D. (1923-2007). Communication Family Theory. Journal of Marital and Family Therapy, 33(3), 291-292.

Johnson, D. H. (1994). Nuer Prophets: A history of prophecy from the Upper Nile in the Nineteenth and Twentieth Centuries. Oxford University Press Inc., New York.

Kapolo, M. T. (2001). Premarital Pastoral Care and Counseling: A Quest for an African Model. Journal of Pastoral Care and Counseling, 1, 2-5. World, Luther Seminary: Saint Paul, Minnesota.

Metz, H. C. (1991). Sudan: A Country Study. Washington, DC: Federal Research Division, Library of Congress.

McFall, E. A. (1970). Approaching the Nuer of Africa Through the Old Testament. Pasadena, California: William Carey Library.

Merriam Webster's Collegiate Dictionary (2002). Merriam -Webster, Incorporated (10th ed). Springfield, Massachussets, U.S.A.

National Marriage Project at Rutgers University (2005). Enrichment Journal on the Divorce rate in America.

O'Neil, D. (2006). Sex and Marriage: An Introduction to the Cultural Rules Regulating Sexual Access and Marriage. Palomar College, San Marcos, CA.

Radcliffe-Brown, A. R., & Forde, D. (1950). African Systems of Kinship and Marriage. Great Britain: Oxford University Press.

Satir, V. (1916-1988). Communication Family Systems Theory. Women's Intellectual Contributions to the Study of Mind and Society. Retrieved July 15, 2011, from http://www.ebster.edu/woolflm/satir.html.

Stone, L. (1997). Kinship and Gender. Boulder, CO, USA: Harper Collins Publishers, Inc.

Sue, D. W., Sue, D. (1990). Counseling the Culturally Different. Theory and Practice (2nd ed.). John Wiley & Sons: New York.

Watchtower Bible and Tract Society of New York (1996). The Secret of Family Happiness. Booklyn: New York, U.S.A.

Zeitzen, M. K. (2008). Polygamy: A Cross-Cultural Analysis. New York, New York, USA: Berg.

Contact

ℰↃ

John Choul Kuek
kuekjohn@yahoo.com

Walter Davis, Jr.
760-917-1251
www.WalterDavisEnterprises.com

www.ingramcontent.com/pod-product-compliance
Lightning Source LLC
Chambersburg PA
CBHW072208280526
45788CB00002B/932